Chinese American Memory
of World War II

Xiaohua Ma

Contents

Preface 1

Introduction 4

I. Chinese Exclusion and American Law 13

II. Chinese Immigration in the Exclusion Era 34

    ⅰ. Angel Island Immigration Station and Chinese Exclusion

    ⅱ. Chinese-American Memory of Angel Island

III. World War II and Chinese Exclusion 47

    ⅰ. Transformation of America's China Policy

    ⅱ. Japan's Racial Propaganda Campaign

    ⅲ. Chinese Exclusion and American Response

IV. Interaction of America's Foreign Policy and Immigration

    Policy 74

    ⅰ. American View of China: Soong May-ling's U.S. Tour

    ⅱ. American Campaign for the Repeal of Chinese Exclusion

Ⅴ. China in America's New World Order ·······················92

    ⅰ. The Strategy of the State Department
    ⅱ. China in America's Postwar Strategy
    ⅲ. Congressional Committee: Toward the Final Repeal

Conclusion ·······················121

Appendix ·······················136

    ⅰ. The Magnuson Act of 1943
    ⅱ. Summary of Chinese Exclusion Acts
    ⅲ. Chronology of Legislative Process of the Repeal of
       the Chinese Exclusion Acts (1943-1944)
    ⅳ. House Resolution 683 of June 18, 2012
    ⅴ. Chinese Population in the United States

Bibliography ·······················154

Preface

On June 18, 2012, U.S. Congress unanimously passed resolution (H. R. 683), which apologized for the passage of the Chinese Exclusion Acts and expressed regret for all the injustice inflicted on Chinese immigrants and Chinese-Americans during the Chinese exclusion period from 1875 to 1943. This resolution was introduced by Chinese-American Congresswoman Judy Chu (Democrat, CA), the first female Chinese-American elected to Congress. It was first introduced as H. R. 282 in May 2011 by Congresswoman Chu with her original co-sponsors, Congressmen Judy Biggert (Republican, IL), Mile Coffman (Republican, CO) and Dana Rohrabacher (Republican, CA). The primary sponsors in the Senate were Senators Scott Brown (Republican, MA) and Dianne Feinstein (Democrat, CA).

Congresswoman Chu made a statement shortly after the resolution was passed on June 18. "The Chinese Exclusion Act enshrined injustice into our legal code - it stopped the Chinese, and the Chinese alone, from immigrating to the United States, from becoming naturalized citizens and even having the right to vote," she said, "The last generation of people personally affected by these laws is leaving us, and finally Congress has expressed the sincere regret that Chinese Americans deserve and reaffirmed our commitment to the civil rights of all people."

Since the Chinese Exclusion Act was enacted by the U.S. Congress in 1882, Chinese entry to the country was strictly prohibited. Chinese immigrants and Chinese-Americans residing in the United States faced severe discrimination and racial prejudice. Many families were split, with wives and children stranded overseas. They had been fighting mechanisms of prejudice, exclusion, and legislative discrimination that prevented them from participating mainstream society during the exclusion period.

The repeal of the Chinese Exclusion Acts in 1943 permitted Chinese immigrants become naturalized citizens. It also allowed a national quota of 105 Chinese immigrants per year. The repeal of the Chinese Exclusion Acts had far reaching significance. From a legal perspective, the repeal of the anti-Chinese immigration legislation marked a historical turning point in American history, since it codified, for the first time, the idea that Chinese immigrants were accepted by American society, despite the fact that the quota granted to them was at first only symbolic. After the repeal of the Chinese Exclusion Acts in 1943, Chinese-Americans continued to fight for legal equality and immigration reform in order to allow family reunification.

Chinese-Americans are a small percentage of the U.S. population, but their numbers are steadily increasing - from 230,000 in 1960 to more than 4 million today. They constitute 1.2% of the total U.S. population according to the 2010 U.S. Census. Chinese-Americans have been the fastest growing group in the United States. They get along well with other racial groups in the United States. Chinese-Americans are highly educated and earn higher incomes when compared to other racial groups in the United

States. The educational achievement of Chinese-Americans are one of the highest among all racial groups in the country. The evolution has been spurred by changes in American immigration policies, labor markets and the increasing economic development of China as well.

The history of Chinese-Americans is the history of dreams, hard-work, prejudice, discrimination, persistence and triumph of the American spirit.

Introduction

It is with particular pride and pleasure that I have today signed the bill repealing the Chinese exclusion acts. The Chinese people, I am sure, will take pleasure in knowing that this represents a manifestation on the part of the American people of their affection and regard....

An unfortunate barrier between allies has been removed. The war effort in the Far East can now be carried on with a greater vigor and a larger understanding of our common purpose.[1]

Franklin D. Roosevelt

These words are taken from President Franklin D. Roosevelt's speech to U.S. Congress made on December 17, 1943, on the occasion of his signing the bill that repealed the Chinese Exclusion Acts. The statement not only demonstrates President Roosevelt's determination to remove the "unfortunate barrier" between the United States and China, but also suggests that a historical transformation of America's China policy had taken place during World War II.

The Chinese Exclusion Acts was the first significant law that restricted immigration into the United States. Many historians and social scientists treated the Chinese Exclusion Acts as a dark and ugly chapter in American history. It also was the first in a series of legislative, executive, and judicial acts by the United States government in the late nineteenth century and early twentieth centuries setting off immigration policy which many scholars consider a racist policy. In the last three or four decades, the Chinese Exclusion Acts has come to be seen as the hinge on which all subsequent American immigration policy turned and the foundation stone of American immigration legislation.

After the enactment of the Chinese Exclusion Act in 1882, historians and social scientists began to examine how the issues of Chinese immigration had affected American politics and legislation. The first scholarly work that focused on the Chinese immigrants in the United States was *Chinese Immigration* (1909), by Mary R. Coolidge.[2] Coolidge's well-documented and detailed analysis became a classic work on Chinese immigration in American history. Her main argument was that the anti-Chinese movement originated in a fund of prejudice combined with economic grievances and specific political circumstances in the 1860-1870s. The movement became even organized in California after 1870, when an economic depression, the division of voting strength between the two major parties, and the labor unrest made Chinese immigration a convenient and expedient issue for labor leaders and politicians. In the 1860s, California labor leaders used the anti-Chinese sentiment of their union members to establish for themselves strong bargaining position and to win political favor from politicians eager to capture the Chinese issue in their quest for votes. As Californian politicians shifted their efforts to achieve restriction from Sacramento to Washington D.C. in the 1870s, the fortuitous circumstances that had allowed "the Chinese Question" to become a politically viable issue in California. Subsequently, the issue began to operate at the national level.

For several decades, Coolidge's study remained the only comprehensive treatment of Chinese immigration in the United States. Her argument of the role of organized labor union in the anti-Chinese movement inspired historians and social scientists for further investigation. In 1975, Elmer Sandmeyer in his book entitled *Anti-Chinese Movement in California* gave a more detailed description of the roles of the labor unions in the West played in the anti-Chinese movement which finally led to the enactment of anti-Chinese laws in the United States Congress.[3]

On the other hand, historians, for example, Alexander Saxton in his book, *The Indispensible Enemy: Labor and the Anti-Chinese Movement in California*, presented a broad study of American ideological history and an intricate examination of the California political system to further a better understanding of the anti-Chinese movement in California from the 1860s to 1902. His work offers a comprehensive study on the ideological origins of the anti-Chinese movement, the political importance of the Chinese problem, the issue's future expansion to include Japanese immigrants.[4] Moreover, Saxton emphasizes the psychological and ideological reasons for the anti-Chinese movement instead of economic and political reasons more commonly used by historians and social scientists.

These studies reevaluate Coolidge's assumptions about the anti-Chinese movement as a phenomenon centered in the West and finally developed throughout the country by the 1870s. This movement dominated by labor organizations catered the political climate. Subsequently, the labor leaders and politicians mad the "Chinese Question" a campaign issue. In sum, the anti-Chinese movement in California in the nineteenth century which led to the Chinese Exclusion Act enacted by U.S. Congress in 1882 was the focus for historians and social scientists.

Meanwhile, a number of important works have supplied ample evidence that Chinese immigration was an important feature of U.S. immigration history and that rather than as passive objects. One of the major studies is Charles McClain's legal history study, *In Search of Equality* published in 1994, which chronicles the nineteenth century conflicts between the Chinese and white American officialdom in California.[5] McClain's research establishes that the Chinese mounted legal challenges to virtually every disadvantage imposed on them by the state of California and the federal government. Many of these cases contributed to the modeling of American constitutional jurisprudence and the formation of immigration policy.

Overall, their research had a profound influence on the historiography of Chinese immigration in the United States. For a long time, scholarship on Chinese immigration has concentrated on the political, economical and ideological reasons that led to the enactment of the Chinese exclusion laws and the formation of American legislation. The issue concerning the repeal of the Chinese Exclusion Acts has been overlooked.

The only study on the repeal of the Chinese Exclusion Acts is Fred R. Rigg's book, *Pressures of Congress: A Study of the Repeal of Chinese Exclusion*, published in 1950.[6] Rigg describes especially the notable work done by a private lobbying group, the Citizens Committee to Repeal the Chinese Exclusion. Rigg's research was based on interviews with U.S. Congressmen, politicians, leaders of the lobbying groups, and officials in the State Department. The book is essentially one on strategy and tactics in coordinating, checkmating and using social and governmental forces to win legislative ends. It is a carefully documented story of the activities of the Citizens' Committee to repeal the Chinese Exclusion Acts.

This case study of the various forces and pressures which culminated in the repeal of the Chinese Exclusion Acts presents the dynamics of political action in American legislative history. It is a valuable study of how public policy and public opinion are formed with an eye on new legislation. Rigg's focus is on the activities of the pressure groups and Congressional debates on the issues of the Chinese immigration, which resulted in the repeal of the Chinese Exclusion Acts in 1943. Because scholarly discussions of the repeal movement relied primarily on Rigg's analysis, the special role of President Franklin D. Roosevelt and his administration has been largely ignored.

However, domestic policy and popular attitudes in the United States intersected with the aim of the U.S. foreign policy in significant way. The Roosevelt administration's China policy and wartime strategy to push the repeal of the Chinese Exclusion Acts through Congress behind the scenes reveal the complex relationship between foreign policy, domestic public opinion, and race relations that shaped the discourse of the repeal movement. As a matter of fact, the repeal required President Roosevelt and his administration to negotiate the competing demands of foreign policy and domestic public opinion, the need to placate China as an ally, and existing racism against Asians, particularly against Japan, America's enemy in East Asia. .

Most importantly, wartime necessity produced the repeal of the Chinese Exclusion Acts in 1943. Matters of foreign policy made it expedient both to embrace a national ideology of equality and to reject racist legislation that affected an ally. As President Roosevelt himself stressed, "there is just one front, which includes at home as well as abroad. It is all part of the picture of trying to win the war."[7] It was a primary aim for Roosevelt to maintain strong relations with China through the war and into the postwar world. Thus all this requires historians to reexamine the nature of America's relations with East Asia, particularly with China during World War II.

Scholarship on U.S.-East Asian relations during World War II has long concentrated on the complexity of political affairs, especially on military strategy, while issues concerning racial equality in international relations have been overlooked. [8] Nevertheless, the war in fact played a critical role in altering America's traditional anti-Chinese policy. It also showed that American immigration policy toward the Asians was overwhelmingly influenced by its foreign policy.

This volume aims to examine how American foreign policy influenced its immigration policy during World War II. It presents the Roosevelt administration's China policy, to treat China as a "Great Power" in American world strategy by repealing the discriminatory laws against Chinese immigrants. It focuses on the repeal of the Chinese Exclusion Acts in 1943. By examining the interaction between American domestic politics and foreign policy, it will enable us to understand that the repeal of the Chinese Exclusion Acts in 1943 not only marked a historical turning point in American immigration policy, but also had a significant impact on the transformation of America's East Asian policy, particularly China policy in the post war era.

Note

[1] Franklin D. Roosevelt's Message to Congress, December 17, 1943, National Archives, Washington D.C.

[2] Mary R. Coolidge, *Chinese Immigration* (New York, 1909).

[3] Elmer Sandmeyer, *The Anti-Chinese Movement in California* (Champaign: University of Illinois Press, 1991).

[4] Alexander Saxton, *The Indispensable Enemy: Labor and the Anti-Chinese Movement in California* (Berkeley: University of California Press, 1975).

[5] Charles McClain, *In Search of Equality: The Chinese Struggle against Discrimination in Nineteenth-Century America* (Berkeley: University of California Press, 1994).

[6] Fred W. Riggs, *Pressures on Congress: A Study of the Repeal of Chinese Exclusion* (New York: King's Crown Press, 1950).

[7] Samuel I. Rosenman, *Working with Roosevelt* (New York, 1952), p.382.

[8] For U.S.-East Asian relations in World War II, see Iriye Akira, *Power and Culture: The Japanese-American War, 1941-1945* (Cambridge: Harvard University Press, 1981), Herbert Feis, *The China Tangle: The American Effort from Pearl Harbor to the Marshall Mission* (Princeton: Princeton University Press, 1953), and Michael Schaller, *The U.S. Crusade in China, 1938-1945* (New York: Columbia University Press, 1979). Racial issues in international relations are mentioned in Christopher Thorne, *Allies of a Kind: The United States, Britain, and the War against Japan, 1941-1945* (London: Hamish Hamilton Ltd, 1982). The best treatment of

racial issue between the United States and Japan is John Dower's book, *War without Mercy: Race and Power in the Pacific War* (New York: Pantheon Books, 1986). However, the racial issue in the China front has been hardly mentioned.

I. Chinese Exclusion and American Law

The first Asian immigrants to enter the United States were Chinese, lured to California by the Gold Rush of 1848. News of the discovery of gold brought thousands of immigrants to California from elsewhere in the United States and from other countries. News of the discovery of gold in the Sancramento Valley in January 1848 reached Hong Kong, a British colony, in the spring and created great excitement. Shipmasters were quick to seize the opportunity, distributing pamphlets concerning the "Golden Mountains."[1] Even today the name of San Francisco is still called "Gold Mountain" in Chinese language.

The most constant and, on the whole, most powerful incentive was the demand for labor in American West. As in all frontier communities, California suffered from labor scarcity, accentuated by the rush to the gold fields. News of the high wages paid to laborers spread all over the world as well as Guangdong Province, southeast China, and drew a large number of Chinese peasants to the American West Coast quite as effectively as the tales of golden marvels.[2]

The Chinese immigrants were mainly rural farmers who left home because of economic and political uncertainty in China. Most of them worked hard and intended to make a lot of money, and then return home as wealthy men. In this goal, the Chinese did not differ from European immigrants who came to the United States in the nineteenth century. The United States experienced a large influx of European immigrants in the nineteen nineteenth century. As Figure 1 illustrates that the United States received approximately nine million immigrants from 1860-1890, while the Chinese constituted only a small amount of the U.S. total immigration population.

Figure 1: Main Sources of Immigration to the U. S. (1861-1890)

Europe	1861-1870	1871-1880	1881-1890
Austria-Hungary	7,800	72,969	353,719
Denmark	17,094	31,771	88,132
France	35,986	72,206	50,464
Germany	787,468	718,182	1,452,970
Great Britain	261,046	525,270	794,549
Ireland	435,778	436,871	655,482
Italy	11,725	55,759	307,309
Norway	71,631	95,323	176,586
Sweden	37,667	115,922	391,776
Switzerland	23,286	28,293	81,988
USSR	2,512	39,284	213,282
Asia			
China	64,301	123,201	61,711
America			
Canada	153,878	383,640	393,304

(Source: Leonard Dinnerstein and David M. Meimers, *Ethnic American: A History of Immigration and Assimilation.* New York: Harper & Row, 1982. Table A.1)

The exodus of Chinese to the United States increased rapidly, from 8 in 1840 to 450 in 1850 and 7,342 in 1860. The construction of the American continental railroad in the 1860s further accelerated the influx of Chinese laborers. The Central Pacific Railroad employed

12,000 Chinese workers by 1868, when they constituted eighty percent of the entire work force. Chinese immigration to the United States peaked at 15,740 in 1870, over ninety percent of whom settled on the Pacific Coast, particularly in California.[3] By 1870, Chinese immigrants made up 30 percent of California's labor force, despite the fact that they constituted only 10 percent of California's total population.

As the number of Chinese increased, many Caucasian workers in California began to resent the Chinese laborers, who might squeeze them out of their jobs. The increasing animosity against Chinese immigrants originated in a variety of concerns and it had widespread effects. The anti-Chinese movement was rooted in a volatile combination of economic, cultural, and racial anxieties on the part of white workers. The Chinese were considered culturally and racially inferior and a threat to American civilization because they were not Christians and thus were unable to be assimilated into the society.

By the 1870s, anti-Chinese sentiment among the white workingmen was spreading among California. Racist labor union leaders directed their actions and the anger of unemployed workers at the Chinese, blaming them for depressed wages and accusing them of being morally corrupted. This view was expressed and reinforced by the stereotypic images of Chinese immigrants recorded in the media of the time. American view of Chinese immigrants focused on aspects of Chinese culture that appeared sinister and exotic to Americans. This image contributed greatly to mass racism and anti-Chinese movement in the nineteenth century America.

Figure 2: American Image of the Chinese

This cartoon titled "The Coming Man" was published in the San Francisco *WASP* approximately one year before the Chinese Exclusion Act was enacted in 1882. "The Coming Man" vividly illustrates the worst in negative stereotyping and Sinophobia. The image appeals to white workingmen's fears of Chinese control of American society and enterprise. Despite the Chinese only occupying 0.002 percent of the U.S. population, visual depictions of the Chinese continued to reinforce imagery of infestation and sinister monopolization of American industry. The stereotypic image of Chinese immigrants in the media strengthened the anti-Chinese hostility in the nineteenth century.

(Source: *The WASP*, May 20, 1881)

By the mid-1870s, the completion of the transcontinental railroad, the growth of the white labor force in the West, particularly in California, and the nationwide economic depression all encouraged white working men to turn against the Chinese. Chinese immigrants encountered prejudice and discrimination that were sometimes manifested in violence. As a consequence of this hostility, in the 1870s, various legal discriminatory measures were taken against the Chinese in California. Ultimately, the anti-Chinese movement helped to foster federal legislation that severely restricted Chinese immigration to the United States.

In response to public demand, the California State Senate and Congress created a special committee to investigate the impact of Chinese immigration in 1876. This investigation of 1876 had helped to solidify anti-Chinese sentiment at the national level. The committee recommended that the measure be taken by the federal government to modify the existing treaties with China so that Congress legislate to restrain the influx of Chinese immigrants. The report was presented to Congress in February 1877 when the contested election of 1876 was being settled, so immediate action was possible. At the same time, the California State Senate suggested the federal government pass legislation regulating the number of Chinese passengers who could be landed by vessel at any U.S. port.[4]

With the development of anti-Chinese sentiment in the Pacific states, particularly in California, a number of bills were introduced in the forty-fifth Congress (1878-1879), requesting the federal government to prohibit Chinese immigration to the United States. House Bill 2143 called for the prohibition of employment of Chinese or Mongolians upon in any public works of the United States. House Bill 2144 aimed to prevent the naturalization of Chinese or Mongolians. Congressman John K. Luttrell (Democrat, California) presented to the House a joint resolution requesting the U.S. government to "use every exertion" to modify all treaties between the United States and China, so the "Chinese immigration to the United States may not be permitted."[5]

Finally they were combined into a so-called the Fifteen Passenger Bill, which permitted only fifteen Chinese passengers to enter the United States on any one vessel docking on the West Coast.[6] While the senators and representatives were debating the bill, Chinese minister Chen Lan-bing in Washington D.C. took immediate steps to stop the restrictive bill. Minister Chen negotiated directly with Secretary of State William Evarts and protested that the bill was a violation of the principle of free emigration provisions in the Burlingame Treaty ratified between China and the United States in 1868. He also suggested President Rutherford R. Hayes veto the bill because it was "offensive and opprobrious" to China.[7]

Figure 3: "The Chinese Must Go"

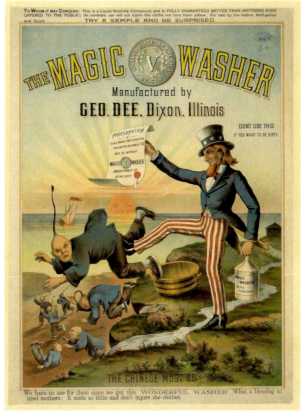

"The Chinese Must Go" was a political slogan of the Workingman's Party in California in the 1870-1880s, led by an Irish immigrant leader Denis Kearney. The movement's goal was to drive the Chinese out of the country. Its political campaign played a significant role in the enactment of the Chinese Exclusion Act of 1882. The visual elements of this poster also support racial stereotype against the Chinese.

(Source: U.S. Library of Congress)

Having received a strong protest from Chinese minister, President Hays vetoed the bill since it violated the free immigration principles of the Burlingame Treaty. President Hayes, however, considered the "Chinese labor invasion" to be "pernicious." He was concerned about public opinion on the Pacific Coast, and favored limiting Chinese immigration by some means consistent with the treaties and recognized international practice. "It should be made certain by proper methods," he wrote in his diary, "that such an invasion can not permanently override our people. It can not safely be admitted to pressure on the bosom of our American society…We would consider with favor measures to discourage the Chinese from coming to our shores."[8]

Responding to the pressure of anti-Chinese sentiment on the Pacific Coast, James B. Angell was appointed special envoy to Beijing to negotiate a new treaty with China. At that time conflicts with Japan concerning the Liuqiu Islands and with Russia about their common border put the Qing government under severe diplomatic pressure. The Qing government compromised, making concession on immigration in order to obtain American assistance with other diplomatic problems. [9] Subsequently, the Angell Treaty was concluded between China and the United States in November 1880, which allowed the United States to "regulate, limit, or suspend, but not absolutely prohibit the immigration of Chinese laborers."[10] On May 6, 1882, the United States Congress enacted a bill prohibiting Chinese immigrants from entering the United States for ten years.[11]

Figure 4: The Chinese Exclusion Act of 1882

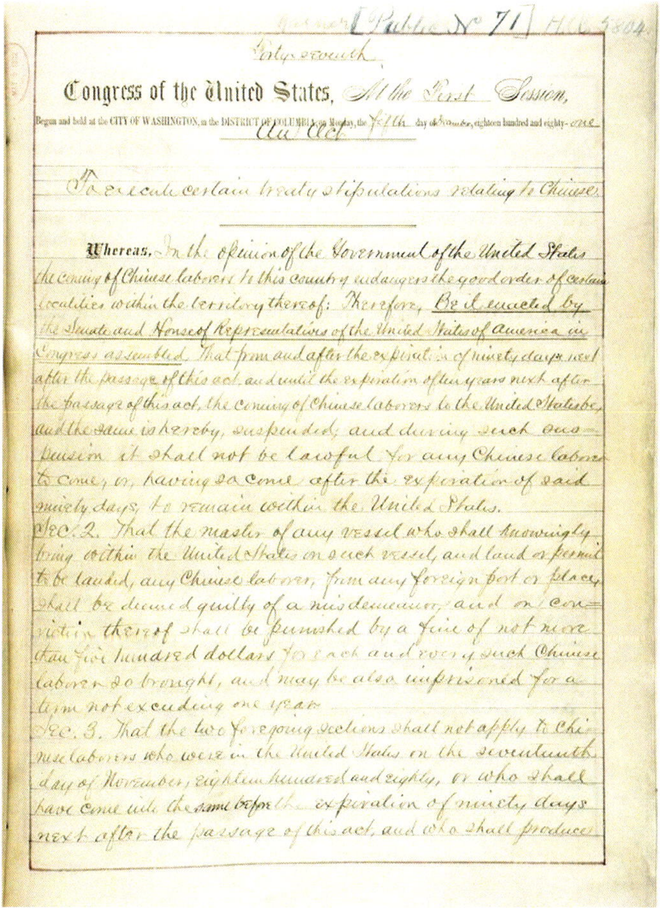

[Public N° 71]

Forty-seventh

Congress of the United States, At the First Session,

Begun and held at the CITY OF WASHINGTON, in the DISTRICT OF COLUMBIA, on Monday, the fifth day of December, eighteen hundred and eighty-one.

An Act

To execute certain treaty stipulations relating to Chinese.

Whereas, In the opinion of the Government of the United States the coming of Chinese laborers to this country endangers the good order of certain localities within the territory thereof: Therefore, Be it enacted by the Senate and House of Representatives of the United States of America in Congress assembled, That from and after the expiration of ninety days next after the passage of this act, and until the expiration of ten years next after the passage of this act, the coming of Chinese laborers to the United States be, and the same is hereby, suspended; and during such suspension it shall not be lawful for any Chinese laborer to come, or, having so come after the expiration of said ninety days, to remain within the United States.

Sec. 2. That the master of any vessel who shall knowingly bring within the United States on such vessel, and land or permit to be landed, any Chinese laborer, from any foreign port or place, shall be deemed guilty of a misdemeanor, and on conviction thereof shall be punished by a fine of not more than five hundred dollars for each and every such Chinese laborer so brought, and may be also imprisoned for a term not exceeding one year.

Sec. 3. That the two foregoing sections shall not apply to Chinese laborers who were in the United States on the seventeenth day of November, eighteen hundred and eighty, or who shall have come into the same before the expiration of ninety days next after the passage of this act, and who shall produce

(Source: U.S. National Archives)

The "Act to Execute Certain Treaty Stipulations Relating to Chinese", namely the Chinese Exclusion Act of 1882, was the first federal immigration legislation to single out an ethnic group by name for invidious treatment. It was the only U.S. law ever to prevent immigration and naturalization on the basis of race.

The Chinese Exclusion Act of 1882 excluded Chinese laborers from entering into the United States for ten years and was the first immigration law passed by Congress. The act was initially intended to last for ten years, but was renewed in 1892 and made permanent in 1902. The emergence of this discriminatory legislation initiated a gradual process of immigration restriction based on race.

On July 5, 1884, the U.S. Congress amended the Chinese Exclusion Act of 1882, which required Chinese to provide an antecedent visa to enter into the United States. Amendments made in 1884 tightened the provisions that allowed previous immigrants to leave and return, and clarified that the legislation applied to ethnic Chinese regardless of their country of origin. The restrictive legislation not only prevented new immigrants but also brought additional suffering for the Chinese as it prevented the reunion of the families of thousands of Chinese immigrants already residing in the United States.

Figure 5: Soong May-ling's Certificate

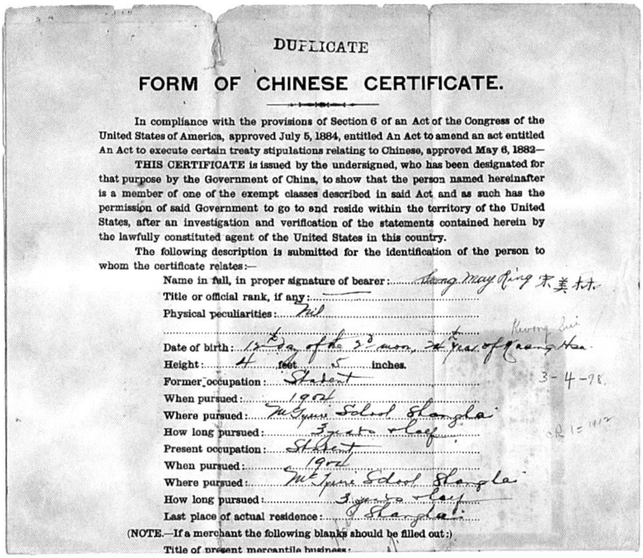

DUPLICATE

FORM OF CHINESE CERTIFICATE.

In compliance with the provisions of Section 6 of an Act of the Congress of the United States of America, approved July 5, 1884, entitled An Act to amend an act entitled An Act to execute certain treaty stipulations relating to Chinese, approved May 6, 1882—

THIS CERTIFICATE is issued by the undersigned, who has been designated for that purpose by the Government of China, to show that the person named hereinafter is a member of one of the exempt classes described in said Act and as such has the permission of said Government to go to and reside within the territory of the United States, after an investigation and verification of the statements contained herein by the lawfully constituted agent of the United States in this country.

The following description is submitted for the identification of the person to whom the certificate relates:—

Name in full, in proper signature of bearer: Soong May Ling 宋美林

Title or official rank, if any: —

Physical peculiarities: Nil

Date of birth: 12th day of the 3rd moon, 24 year of Kwang Hsu

Height: 4 feet 5 inches.

Former occupation: Student

When pursued: 1904

Where pursued: McTyeire School Shanghai

How long pursued: 3 years & half

Present occupation: Student

When pursued: 1904

Where pursued: McTyeire School Shanghai

How long pursued: 3 years & half

Last place of actual residence: Shanghai

(NOTE.—If a merchant the following blanks should be filled out:)

Title of present mercantile business:

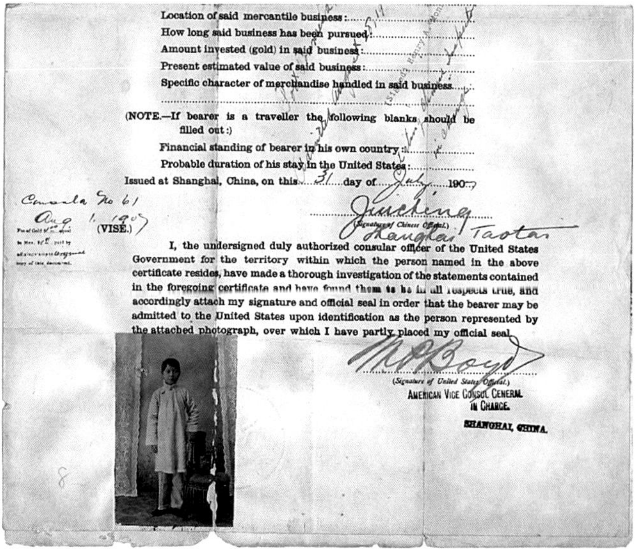

Location of said mercantile business:

How long said business has been pursued:

Amount invested (gold) in said business:

Present estimated value of said business:

Specific character of merchandise handled in said business:

(NOTE.—If bearer is a traveller the following blanks should be filled out:)

Financial standing of bearer in his own country:

Probable duration of his stay in the United States:

Issued at Shanghai, China, on this 31 day of July 1907

Jiucheng
(Signature of Chinese Official.)
Shanghai Taotai

(VISÉ.)

I, the undersigned duly authorized consular officer of the United States Government for the territory within which the person named in the above certificate resides, have made a thorough investigation of the statements contained in the foregoing certificate and have found them to be in all respects true, and accordingly attach my signature and official seal in order that the bearer may be admitted to the United States upon identification as the person represented by the attached photograph, over which I have partly placed my official seal.

W. P. Boyd
(Signature of United States Official.)
AMERICAN VICE CONSUL GENERAL IN CHARGE.
SHANGHAI, CHINA.

From 1882 to 1943 the United States severely curtained immigration from China. The Chinese Exclusion Act also required every Chinese person traveling or out of the country to carry a certificate identifying his or her status as a laborer, student, scholar, merchant or diplomat. The certificate for Soong May-ling (future wife of Chiang Kai-shek) was issued on July 31, 1907 to certify her purpose to study in the United States.

(Source: U.S. National Archives, Washington D.C.)

On October 1, 1888, U.S. Congress enacted the Scott Act, which prohibited Chinese immigrants from returning to the United States after visiting China. This restrictive legislation made Chinese reentry to the United States after a visit to China impossible, even for long-term legal residents. Despite strong protest from China, the U.S. government extended and strengthened the Chinese Exclusion Act in 1892 by adding numerous new requirements, also known as the Geary Act. The Geary Act banned unskilled laborers and only allowed students, teachers, merchants, diplomats and travelers for pleasure and curiosity as "exempt classes" to enter into the United States.

Furthermore the restrictive legislation required Chinese who lived in the United States to register and secure a certificate as proof of their right to enter the United States.[12] At the same time, anti-miscegenation laws in many states prohibited Chinese men from marrying white women.[13]

Figure 6: Certificate of Residence for Chinese in the U.S.

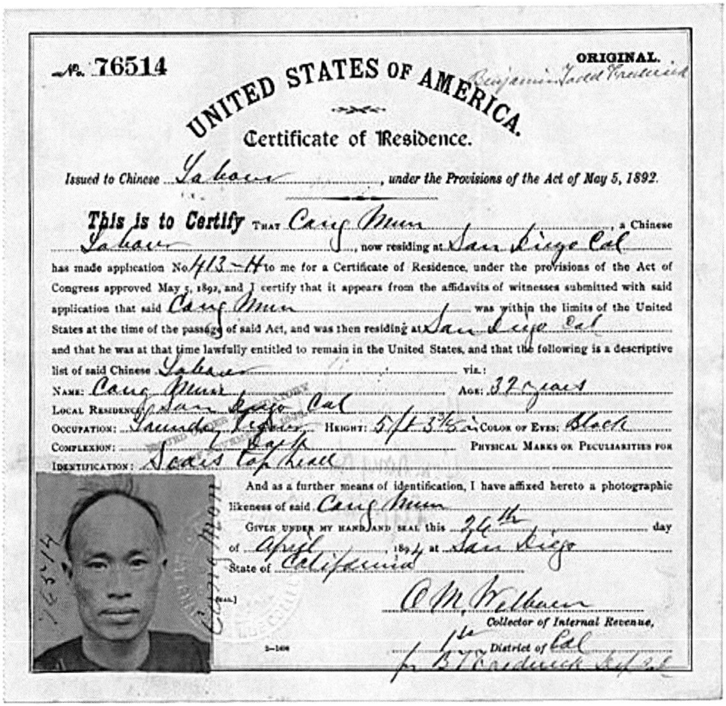

No. 76514 ORIGINAL.

UNITED STATES OF AMERICA.

Certificate of Residence.

Issued to Chinese Laborer, under the Provisions of the Act of May 5, 1892.

This is to Certify That Cang Mun, a Chinese Laborer, now residing at San Diego Cal has made application No. 413-H to me for a Certificate of Residence, under the provisions of the Act of Congress approved May 5, 1892, and I certify that it appears from the affidavits of witnesses submitted with said application that said Cang Mun was within the limits of the United States at the time of the passage of said Act, and was then residing at San Diego Cal and that he was at that time lawfully entitled to remain in the United States, and that the following is a descriptive list of said Chinese Laborer viz.:

Name: Cang Mun Age: 32 years

Local Residence: San Diego Cal

Occupation: Laundry Height: 5 ft 3 Color of Eyes: Black

Complexion: Dark Physical Marks or Peculiarities for Identification: Scars top head

And as a further means of identification, I have affixed hereto a photographic likeness of said Cang Mun.

Given under my hand and seal this 26th day of April, 1894, at San Diego State of California

[SEAL.]

O. M. Welburn
Collector of Internal Revenue,
1st District of Cal

The Chinese residing the United States faced new requirements under the Chinese Exclusion Act of 1882. The act required each Chinese to register and obtain a certificate of residence. This certificate was issued on April 26, 1894, for a Chinese immigrant. Chinese immigrants were the only racial group to be severely controlled and discriminated legally.

(Source: U.S. National Archives, Washington D.C.)

The exclusion laws and the racism had a profound and

far-reaching effect on the Chinese-American community in the United States. In 1884, a California court interpreted the 1882 Exclusion Act to mean that Chinese immigrants could not send for their wives. As a result, families were separated for years, or even decades. Children grew up without their fathers, and in the rural villages of China and the early Chinatowns of America, countless wives and husbands were sentenced to lonely and separate lives. This enforced separation stunted the normal development of both family life and community organizations. Chinese immigrants suffered from unfair treatments from society. In the meantime, racial prejudices and social isolation prevented their interaction with mainstream society.

Moreover, the enactment of the exclusion acts marked the end of the free immigration era in American history. These discriminatory acts not only had long-term repercussions for America's relations with China, but also affected overall immigration policy and internal politics. On the other hand, it can also be considered as merely one step in the growth of anti-Asian immigration legislation.

Following enactment of the Chinese Exclusion Act in 1882, Asian immigrants became a constant target of American nativism and racism. Increased agitation for a more effective law reached a climax after World War I when the quota act of 1921 was enacted, introducing the quantitative principle of immigration restriction. Under the pressure of economic depression, the Immigration Act of 1921, also known as the National Origins Act, provided that the number of immigrants from any country during a fiscal year should not exceed three percent of the number of persons born in that country and resident in the United States in 1910. The act controlled "undesirable" immigrants by establishing quotas. Based on the Naturalization Acts of 1790 and 1870, only people of white or African descent were eligible for naturalization. Moreover, the act forbade further immigration from Asian countries ineligible to be naturalized.

The U.S. congress enacted the Johnson-Reed Act in 1924. The new law limited the number of immigrants allowed entry into the United States through a national origins quota. The quota provided immigration visas to two percent of the total number of people of each nationality in the United States as of the 1890 national census but immigrants from Asian countries were completely excluded.[14] Subsequently, the Immigration Act of 1924 closed the door on any further immigration from Asian countries.

Figure 7: Chinese Student Certificate

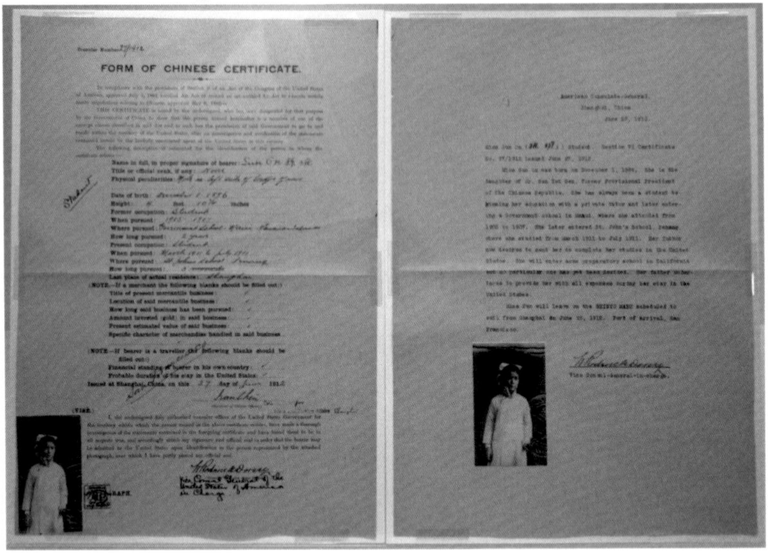

FORM OF CHINESE CERTIFICATE.

Name in full, in proper signature of bearer:
Title or official rank, if any:
Physical peculiarities:
Date of birth:
Height: feet inches
Former occupation:
When pursued:
Where pursued:
How long pursued:
Present occupation:
When pursued:
Where pursued:
How long pursued:
Last place of actual residence:
(NOTE.—If a merchant the following blanks should be filled out:)
Title of present mercantile business:
Location of said mercantile business:
How long said business has been pursued:
Amount invested (gold) in said business:
Present estimated value of said business:
Specific character of merchandise handled in said business:
(NOTE.—If bearer is a traveller the following blanks should be filled out:)
Financial standing of bearer in his own country:

(Source: Dr. Sun Yat-sen Museum, Hong Kong)

Figure 7 is a sample of Chinese Student Certificate issued on June 27, 1912. This certificate with a special note from American Vice Consulate-General in Shanghai was for the founder of the Republic of China, Dr. Sun Yat-sen's daughter, Sun On (孫琬, later Sun Wan) to enter to the United States. After the Geary Act was enacted in 1892, the situation for the Chinese in the United States became extremely difficult. This certificate demonstrates the difficulty for the Chinese to enter to the United States. It states:

Form of Chinese Certificate

In compliance with the provisions of Section 6 of an Act of the Congress of the United States of America, approved July 5, 1884, entitled An Act to amend An Act to execute certain treaty stipulations relating to Chinese, approved May 6, 1882. -

This Certificate is issued by the undersigned, who has been designated for that purpose by the Government of China, to show that the person named hereinafter is a member of one of the exempt classes described in said Act and as such has the permission of said Government to go to and reside within the territory of the United States, after an investigation and verification of the statements contained herein by the lawfully constituted agent of the United States in this country.

The following description is submitted for the identification of the person to whom the certificate relates:

Name in full, in proper signature of bearer: Sun On (孫琬)

Title or official rank, if any: None

Physical peculiarities:

Date of Birth: September 1, 1896

Height: 4 feet 10 3/4 inches

Former Occupation: Student

......

American Consulate-General

Shanghai, China, 1912

Miss Sun On (孫琬) student

Section VI Certificate

No.27/1912 issued June 27, 1912

Miss Sun On was born on December 1, 1896. She is the daughter of Mr. Sun Yat Sen, former Provisional President of the Chinese Republic. She has always been a student beginning her education with a private tutor and later entering a Government School in Maui, where she attended from 1905 to 1907. She later entered St. John's School, Penang, where she studied from March 1911 to July 1911. Her father now desires to send her to complete her studies in the United States. She will enter some preparatory school in California but no particular one has yet been decided. Her father undertakes to provide her with all expenses during her stay in the United States.

Miss Sun will leave the SHINYO MARU scheduled to sail from Shanghai on June 28, 1912. Port of Arrival, San Francisco.

Vice Consul-General-in-Charge

American Consulate-General (Signature)

June 27, 1912

Note

[1] Paul Yee, *Tales from Gold Mountain: Stories of the Chinese in the New World* (Toronto: Greenwood Books, 2003).

[2] For the Gold Rush in California, see Elizabeth Raum, *The California Gold Rush: An Interactive History Adventure* (Mankato: Minnesota: Capstone Press, 2007); Mel Friedman, *The California Gold Rush* (New York: Children's Press, 2010).

[3] For Chinese immigration, see Shih-Shan Henry Tsai, *The Chinese Experience in America* (Bloomington: Indiana University Press, 1986), and Elliott Yong, *Alien Nation: Chinese Migration in the Americas from Coolie Era through World War II* (Chapel Hills: North Carolina University Press, 2014).

[4] Charles J. McClain, *In Search of Equality: The Chinese Struggle Against Discrimination in Nineteenth-Century America*, p.146.

[5] Shih-shan Henry Tsai, *China and the Overseas Chinese in the United States, 1868-1911* (Fayetteville: University of Arkansas Press, 1983), p.45.

[6] Charles J. McClain, *In Search of Equality: The Chinese Struggle Against Discrimination in Nineteenth-Century America*, pp.146-147; Martin B. Gold, *Forbidden Citizens: Chinese Exclusion and the U.S. Congress: A Legislative History* (Washington D.C.: TheCapitol.Net, 2012).

[7] Shih-shan Henry Tsai, *China and the Overseas Chinese in the United States, 1868-1911*, p.46.

[8] T. Harry Williams, ed., *Hayes: The Diary of a President, 1875-1881* (New

York, 1964), pp.187-88, and p.192.

[9] Shih-shan Henry Tsai, *China and the Overseas Chinese in the United States, 1868-1911*, pp.46-47, and Wu Ju-lun, ed., *Li weng zhong gon quanji* [Complete Works of Li Hong-zhang] Vol. 8, (Taibei, 1962), pp.207-209.

[10] Shih-shan Henry Tsai, *China and the Overseas Chinese in the United States, 1868-1911*, pp.58-59.

[11] For the formation of the Chinese Exclusion Act of 1882, see Andrew Gyory, *Closing the Gate: Race, Politics and the Chinese Exclusion Act* (Chapel Hills: University of North Carolina Press, 1998).

[12] The Chinese Exclusion Act of 1882 was extended for ten years. It was also known as the Geary Act (An Act to Prohibit the Coming of Chinese Persons into the United States of May 1892). The United States Congress renewed the Geary Act in 1902 and enacted a number of anti-Chinese immigration laws after the Chinese Exclusion Act in 1882. There had been fifteen discriminatory laws against the Chinese in American immigration legislation until 1913. Generally they are called the Chinese Exclusion Acts. For the legislative process of the Chinese Exclusion Acts, see Le Tien-lu, *Congress Policy on Chinese Immigration* (New York: Arno Press, 1978).

[13] Chin Gabriel and Hrishi Karthikeyan, "Preserving Racial Identity: Population Patterns and Application or Anti-Miscegenation Statutes to Asian Americans, 1910-1950, *Asian Law Journal,* Vol.19, 2002, pp.1-35.

[14] For the enactment of the Johnson-Reed Act of 1924, see Herbert P. Lepore, *Anti-Asian Exclusion in the United States during the Nineteenth Century and the Twentieth Centuries: The History Leading to the*

Immigration Act of 1924 (Lewiston, New York: Edwin Mellen Press, 2013).

II. Chinese Immigration in the Exclusion Era

Angel Island Immigration Station, also known as the "Ellis Island of the West" was constructed in 1905 in an area known as China Cove, San Francisco and was finally put into operation in 1910. It was primarily produced to enforce the Chinese Exclusion Acts enacted by the U.S. Congress in 1882. This facility was created to control the flow of Chinese immigrants' entry to the United States. It was necessary after the implementation of the Chinese Exclusion Acts. Between 1910 and 1940, Chinese immigrants were detained at the Angle Island Immigration Station where they were required to undergo humiliating medical examinations and various detailed interrogations.

Between 1890 and 1924, over 20 million immigrants entered the United States, more than in any comparable period in American history. Fleeing poverty and oppression for a better life, many immigrants never forgot their first glimpse of the Statue of Liberty besides the Ellis Island. Holding aloft a welcoming torch, she symbolized America's promise, a land of freedom. In the words inscribed at the statue's base, "Give me your tired, your poor, your huddled masses yearning to breathe free." These words mythologized the experience for European immigrants who entered the gateway of the East Coast: Ellis Island Immigration Station in New York Harbor.

In contrast, the majority of immigrants arriving in San Francisco received a much chillier reception at the remote Angel Island

Immigration Station. Because of the anti-Asian immigration acts, immigration officials in Angel Island devoted themselves to keeping newcomers out of the United States, rather than welcoming them in. The Angel Island Immigration Station served as the West Coast port of entry for Asian immigrants arriving in the United States. Between 1910 and 1940 it is estimated that 250,000 Chinese and 150,000 Japanese immigrants were processed through the Angel Island Immigration Station.[1]

The station also functioned as an interrogation and detention center during the height of national hostility toward Chinese and other Asians seeking new lives in the United States. The majority of immigrants crossing the Pacific came from Asia, mostly from China and Japan, not Europe. The legislative and political process of the Chinese Exclusion Acts has been well examined. Nevertheless, less is known about the enforcement of the Chinese Exclusion Acts in the Angel Island Immigration Station.

i. Angel Island Immigration Station and Chinese Exclusion

In the early twentieth century, most of Chinese immigrants coming to the United States were detained at the Angel Island Immigration Station. The detention facility was considered ideal because of its isolated location, making it easy to control immigrants, enforce the new restrictive immigration laws as well as any outbreaks of disease. The predominantly Chinese immigrants who were detained at the facility were denied entry to the country. The interrogation process was long. Chinese immigrants were detained weeks, months, sometimes even years. Many of them confronted racial discrimination and received unfair treatments there.

Figure 8: A Bird View of Angel Island Immigration Station

(Photograph by Xiaohua Ma)

The most visible and enduring testament of Chinese experience in the Angel Island Immigration Station are the poems, some written with pencil or brush, others carved using a classical Chinese technique, deep into the wooden walls of the barracks. Long dismissed as mere graffiti, these poems are a vital historic record of the aspirations of Chinese immigrants, and of their anger and sadness at the injustice of their initial reception in America.

While waiting for entry into the United States, many Chinese newcomers at Angel Island began carving poetry in the walls of their barracks. Many detained expressed their fears, despair and frustrations in poetry written and carved into the barrack walls in Chinese language. Some poems are still visible today.

Figure 9: Chinese Poems Carved in the Wall

The detention center bears witness to the bitterness and frustration of excluded Chinese immigrants who carved more than one hundred poems into the barrack walls. The picture above is one corner of the barrack walls. It illustrates the

loneliness and anxiety of the Chinese at the detention center.
(Photograph by Xiaohua Ma)

One poem writes:

"Retained in this wooden house for several weeks
Because of the exclusion law
It is pity even for a hero like me
I can do nothing here
No opportunity to explain
I have to wait and wait......"

Figure 10: Chinese Poems Carved on Wall of a Detention Barrack

Many carvings and writings have been found on the barrack walls of the detention center in the Angel Island Immigration Station. The writings and carvings express Chinese immigrants' thoughts and feelings, hopes, sorrow, anger and despair. They were rediscovered in 1970 and have been preserved today.
(Photograph by Xiaohua Ma)

The Chinese made up most of the detainees. The immigration officials gave different treatment to different countries. Because of the exclusion acts, the Chinese newcomers were detained in the Angel Island Immigration Station much longer than other groups and confronted humiliating treatment.[2]

Figure 11: The Detention Center

(Photograph by Xiaohua Ma)

The predominantly Chinese immigrants who were detained at Angel Island were not welcomed in the United States. Many of the detainees turned to poetry as expression. They spilled their emotions onto the walls that contained them. These etchings remain on the walls of the detention center of the Angel Island Immigration Station today as poignant reminders of Chinese experience and an unjust time in American history.

Figure 12: One Corner of Angel Island Immigration Station

Hopeful Chinese immigrants were confined in this isolated

detention center after entering the United States, a promised land. (Photograph by Xiaohua Ma)

In 1941, following the departure of the Immigration Service from the island, the station property was returned to the U.S. Army, and it became the North Garrison of Fort McDowell. After Japan attacked the American military base at Pearl Harbor on December 7, 1941, the United States entered World War II. The old immigration barracks became a Prisoner of War Processing Center. Japanese and German prisoners were processed there before being sent to permanent camps in the interior.

Figure 13: Chinese Dormitory in the Detention Center

The Chinese were confined in these segregated dormitories during the long interrogation process.

(Photograph by Xiaohua Ma)

ⅱ. Chinese-American Memory of Angel Island

Since U.S. Congress repealed the Chinese Exclusion Acts in 1943, the facility was closed as an immigration station. The Angel Island Immigration Station became a symbol of the historical injustices suffered by Asian immigrants, especially Chinese immigrants in the early twentieth century. Approximately one million Asian immigrants were processed and detained there between 1910 and 1940.

In 1970s, Chinese-Americans established the Angel Island Immigration Station Historical Advisory Committee to preserve the and restore the site. Due to their continuous endeavors, California passed a special legislation providing $250,000 for preserving the detention barracks and the Chinese poetry in the barracks walls at the station.[3] To raise awareness of the experience of immigrants into the United States through the Pacific, Angel Island Immigration Station Foundation was founded in 1983. The purpose of the foundation is to serve as a symbol of American willingness to learn from their past to ensure that the nation keeps its promise of liberty and freedom.[4] On December 9, 1997, the Angel Island Immigration Station was designated as a National Historic Landmark District by the federal government.

The detention center was renovated and reopened to the public on February 16, 2009. At Angel Island, a museum has been established in the old barracks, recreating one of the living areas for Chinese detainees. Today Angle Island becomes a national historical landmark for people to learn about the past of American people.

Figure 14: The Angel Island Bell

The bronze liberty bell displayed outside of the detention center symbolizes the spirit of the United States.
(Photograph by Xiaohua Ma)

On January 20, 2010, President Barrack Obama visited Angel Island to commemorate the 100 year anniversary of Angel Island

Immigration Station's opening. On January 21, 2010, National Angel Island Day was proclaimed by President Obama. The day is meant to honor all those immigrants who "endured so many hardships" and suffered "racially prejudiced" treatments at the detention center before being allowed to enter the country.[5] It has become a symbol for Chinese-Americans to fight for equality in the United States.

Figure 15: Immigrant Heritage Wall at Angel Island

Many decades have passed after the Chinese Exclusion Acts were repealed in 1943. But many Chinese still recall the hardship of detention. The Immigrant Heritage Wall is a memorial to those who made difficult journeys across the Pacific to endure weeks, sometimes months, or even years, of anxiety and despair as they were detained and interrogated immediately after entering the country. Inscribed upon the plaques are the names of hundreds of Chinese immigrants and their descendents.

(Photograph by Xiaohua Ma)

Note

[1] The data is from "U.S. Immigration Station, Angel Island: San Francisco Bay, California,"
http://www.nps.gov/nr/travel/Asian_American_and_Pacific_Islander_Heritage/US-Immigration-Station-Angel-Island.htm.
For the activities of Chinese-Americans for preserving the historical site of the Angel Island Immigration Station, see, "Angel Island Immigrant Journey," Angel Island Immigration Foundation, 2004.
http://www.aiisf.org/education/station-history.

[2] Robert Barde and Gustavo J. Bobonis, "Detention at Angel Island: First Empirical Evidence," *Social Science History,* Vol.30, 2006, p.130.

[3] "Immigration Station," California Department of Parks and Recreation, http://www.parks.ca.gov/?page_id=1309.

[4] For the purpose of Angel Island Immigration Station Foundation, see its homepage: http://www.aiisf.org/.

[5] "Presidential Proclamation: National Angel Island Day," by President Barrack Obama on January 20, 2010, the White House release.
https://www.whitehouse.gov/the-press-office/presidential-proclamation-national-angel-island-day.

III. World War II and Chinese Exclusion

America's restrictive immigration policy, which excluded aliens defined by race, did not change until after Japan's attack at Pearl Harbor on December 7, 1941. The sudden attack led directly to a crucial transformation of America's Asian policy.

Immediately after the attack, President Roosevelt signed a presidential proclamation permitting the apprehension of any alien Japanese "deemed dangerous to the public peace or safety of the United States."[1] Although Kido Saburo, president of the Japanese-American Citizens League, in a radio address the next day claimed that Japanese Americans were "loyal to America," agents of the Federal Bureau of Investigation picked up hundreds of Japanese Americans.[2] As a result, approximately 120,000 men, women, and children of Japanese ancestry were evicted from the West Coast of the United States and held in internment camps across the country. Subsequently, many of them were drafted into the U.S. army in order to test their "loyalty" to the United States.[3]

In contrast to the deterioration in U.S. relations with Japan, the war united China and the United States. The day after the attack, the United States together with China declared war on Japan, and the two countries became allies immediately. The special wartime alliance between China and the United States resulted in a shift of America's East Asian policy, especially its policy towards China.

ⅰ. **Transformation of America's China Policy**

Traditionally, America's China policy had been based on the Open Door doctrine, which sought to maintain the balance of power in East Asia while pursuing commercial interests in China. The essence of this policy did not include defending China's independence and sovereignty. During World War I, the Chinese were disappointed by President Woodrow Wilson's policy towards China. Throughout the 1920s, the United States failed to give any effective support to Dr. Sun Yat-sen and the Chinese nationalist movement. In the 1930s, America's policy of appeasement towards Japan led it to sacrifice the interest of China. Typical of this policy was Henry L. Stimson's non-recognition policy toward Japan's occupation of Northeast China; the United States made every effort to avoid involvement in the Sino-Japanese War.

Nevertheless, as Japan's aggression in China became more widespread, the United States became anxious about the crisis in China, as Japanese troops were occupying most areas of China and menaced vital American interests in Asia. In November 1940, as soon as Japan recognized the Wang Jing-wei puppet regime in Nanjing, the United States responded vigorously by offering lend-lease aid to Chiang Kai-shek. However, the crucial transformation of America's China policy did not occur until late 1941, after Japan's sudden attack at Pearl Harbor.

Upon hearing of the attack, Chiang Kai-shek immediately summoned the American Ambassador to China, Clarence Gauss, and proposed a military alliance of Allied nations to fight against the Powers.[4] On December 13, Secretary of State Cordell Hull instructed Maxwell M. Hamilton, Chief of the Division of Far Eastern Affairs of the State Department, "to draw up a draft of a declaration to be made by the nations fighting the Axis, which would bind them together until victory and would commit them to the basic principles that we uphold."[5] On January 1, 1942, a Joint Declaration of the United Nations was issued, with China listed as the fourth signatory, following the United States, Great Britain, and the Soviet Union.[6] The inclusion of China as a major power in the declaration demonstrated that China had become indispensable to America's war strategy.

In the early part of the war, however, the United States adopted a "Europe First Policy." This policy implied that the war in Asia was secondary in America's global strategy. Although the outbreak of the Pacific War altered American concerns and forced the United States to focus on the war in Asia, Washington's primary aim was to "keep China in the war" in order to tie up millions of Japanese troops until the ultimate Allied victory in Europe. As Stanley K. Hornbeck, Adviser to the Secretary of State Cordell Hull, pointed out when the United States decided to lend China five hundred million dollars in January 1942, it was "the time for us to tie China into our war (which still is her war) as tight as possible."[7]

For the United States, China's importance in the war was twofold. America intended to make use of Chinese resistance forces to fight against the Japanese aggressors. Meanwhile, from the perspective of

49

America's own military strategy, bases on the Chinese mainland would permit American bombers to strike Japan. Admiral Harry E. Yarnell, former Commander in Chief of the U.S. Asiatic Fleet, testified in House Committee that the Chinese mainland was "the only area from which long-range bombers can reach Japan."[8] This led to the conclusion that Allied success against Japan required the continued participation of China in the war.

Figure 16: America's Image of China

This 1942 poster, titled "This Man Is Your Friend - Chinese, He

Fights for Freedom," widely circulated in the United States following the Japanese attack on Pearl Harbor. Its purpose was to support China in the war against the Japanese aggression.

(Source: Franklin D. Roosevelt Library)

By early 1943, the United States had begun developing concrete plans for using Chinese bases as the launching pad for an air offensive against Japan. In March, President Roosevelt suggested organizing a five-hundred-plane air force in China for launching air attacks. [9] Thus the continuation of Chinese resistance and cooperation was certainly an important American objective.

In order to achieve this goal, the United States attempted to buttress China. Politically, one of the most important measures taken was to aid China's participation in international affairs, promoting China as a "Great Power" on the world stage. This strategy emerged in the spring of 1942. On May 2, 1942, President Roosevelt declared that "in the future an unconquerable China will play its proper role in maintaining peace and prosperity not only in Eastern Asia but in the whole world." [10] Soon after, in discussions with Soviet Foreign Minister V. M. Molotov in May – June 1942, Roosevelt emphasized the importance of postwar cooperation among the "four policemen," which included China together with the United States, Great Britain, and the Soviet Union. [11] In December 1942, in a conversation with Owen Lattimore, former American special adviser to Chiang Kai-shek, Roosevelt stressed the role of China as a member of the "Big Four" after the war. [12]

Moreover, the treaty concluded with China on January 11, 1943, to relinquish American extraterritorial rights in China, further demonstrated that the United States intended to give formal expression to China's "Great Power" status.[13] This special alliance, however, did not alter the racially unequal relations that existed between the United States and China. The continuing existence of the Chinese Exclusion Acts was one example of this unaltered inequality. Thus, America's racially discriminatory immigration laws became a vital resource for Japan in its campaign of "Asia for the Asiatics."

ⅱ. Japan's Racial Propaganda Campaign

Soon after the outbreak of the Pacific War, another front, which used propaganda, started. On this battlefield to establish a new world order, the conflicts between the United States and Japan became rather aggravated as the war expanded. Even before the war broke out, Japan had targeted Western imperialism, appealing to other Asian countries to cooperate with Japan to construct "Asia for the Asiatics."

Five days after the attack on Pearl Harbor, Japan began to call the war "The Greater East Asia War" and proclaimed that its war aim was to "overthrow the American and British imperialists, who have oppressed and squeezed one billion Asians, in order to establish an ideal order of co-prosperity and co-existence in East Asia." [14] Meanwhile, Japanese propagandists utilized "psychological weaponry," emphasizing the discriminatory policy of the Chinese

52

Exclusion Acts, to fight against Roosevelt's Four Freedom, from which racial equality was excluded.

To reinforce the propaganda effect, in early February 1942, with the guidance of the Japanese army, *FRONT*, one of the most important wartime propaganda magazines, began publication, condemning Western oppression in Asia and extolling "racial harmony" in "the Greater East Asia Co-Prosperity." In February 1942, an article entitled "A New Step towards the Emancipation of Asiatics" appeared in *Toa Kaihou* [Emancipation of East Asia]. It proclaimed that the essence of "injustice and inequality" was rooted in the American exploitation of "the yellow race."[15]

Later, in June 1942, a series of "Open Letters to Asian Peoples" came out in the *Asahi Shimbun*, in which exploitation and oppression of Asian peoples by the Anglo-Saxon Powers was strongly denounced.[16] Furthermore, in another editorial entitled "Shake Hands – Japan and China" appearing on June 25 in the *Asahi Shimbun*, the author accused Western democracies of hypocrisy and appealed to the Chinese people to "share hardship with the Japanese in the Greater East Asia War" which aimed to fight for "China's independence and freedom."[17]

By 1943, Japanese government launched a special propaganda attack on America's discriminatory laws against the colored people. In January, Japan formulated "A Propaganda Strategy Overseas for the Racial Issues," in which Japan proclaimed that its war purpose was to set free the colored people who had been exploited by American imperialists for centuries. The focus of this strategy was to utilize the racial discrimination against the black and Asian people to fight against American racism.

The Japanese propaganda campaign was not only directed toward the United States, Great Britain, and other western imperialist countries, but also towards Asian countries whom they sought to conquer. During wartime, Japan began studying about the culture and customs of their Western counterparts. In many ways, Japan took on many of the ideas and methods of American expansionism, and, consciously or subconsciously, incorporated them into their own methods of conquest throughout Asia.

On the other hand, the Japanese propaganda campaign emphasized that Japan's victory would contribute to the liberation of the "colored people" in the world.[18] Japanese propagandists claimed that equality slogans from the United States were "hypocritical" and that the essence of "so-called equality" was the "beast-like treatment or semi-starvation pay to the Asian peoples."[19] "Asia must be one - in her aim, in her future," Japanese propaganda proclaimed: "when Asia becomes one in truth, a new order will be established throughout the world."[20] In summary, the Japanese propagandists ridiculed the Allied Powers in their newspapers and radio propaganda directed towards Asian peoples, insinuating that Asian peoples would never receive equal and impartial treatment from the Allied Powers.

Words are powerful, but some of the images in wartime cartoons and posters drew attention more vividly because they attracted an audience on a wide scale. The cartoon propaganda is powerful and often a silent weapon that targets human emotions and psyches.

Cartoons are driven by human emotions and impulses more easily and further than the politics and military actions. Figure 17 is a wartime Japanese cartoon which illustrates vividly that Japan had successfully overthrown Anglo-American imperialism in East Asia.

Figure 17: Japanese Cartoon
"The Tentacles of Imperialism Have Been Cut"

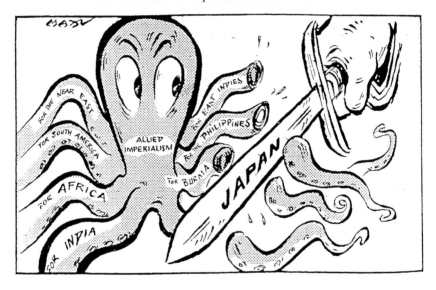

Propaganda is usually defined as biased information intended to promote a particular political cause or view. Wartime Japanese propaganda was a reaction against the Anglo-Saxon domination in the word. During the war, "Asian for the Asiatics" was a widespread slogan for Japan to attack Western imperialism. Japanese propaganda appealed to occupied countries to cooperate with Japan in order to establish "the Greater East Asia

Co-prosperity Sphere."

(Source: *The Times Weekly*, June 28, 1943)

One of the most important reasons for the enactment of the Chinese Exclusion Act in 1882 had been American racism, or the sense of white superiority, which was firmly rooted in the ideology of social Darwinism and late nineteenth-century American nativism. This dominant ideology became the critical factor in the exclusion not only for the Chinese, but also for all Asian races. While explaining the universality of the Atlantic Charter in his address on Memorial Day, 1942, Under Secretary of State, Sumner Welles insisted that "the discrimination between peoples because of their race, creed or color must be abolished."[21] Nevertheless, the racially discriminatory laws against Asians, particularly Chinese, still existed at that time in American legislation.

As mentioned above, the alliance between China and the United States was established as soon as the Pacific War broke out, because China, according to President Roosevelt, was "the first to stand up and fight against aggression in this war."[22] This special alliance, however, did not alter the unequal relations both internationally and racially that existed between the two countries. The continuing existence of the Chinese Exclusion Acts was one example of this unaltered inequality.

Under these circumstances, Japanese propagandists found valuable ammunition for their appeals to other Asians and began to use this "weaponry" to fight against the Allied Powers, pursing a campaign of "Asia for the Asiatics" since China was not treated as equally as other Allied Powers in American legislation.

Figure 18: "Melting Under the Rising Sun"

Propaganda is used to influence people psychologically in order to alter social perceptions. This cartoon, titled "Anglo-Saxon Prestige and Power Melting Under the Rising Sun," reinforced the idea that under the leadership of Japan, a new order to ensure the stability and prosperity of the world free from Western exploitation and imperialism would be established.

(Source: *The Time Weekly*, March 21, 1943)

As the 100th anniversary of the ratification of the Nanjing Treaty, the first unequal treaty signed between China and the Western Powers, approached, the Japanese government decided to make full use of this opportunity to condemn British and American imperialism and their brutal invasions in Asia. On August 17, 1942, Shigemitsu Mamoru, Japanese Ambassador to Nanjing, sent a confidential telegram to the Foreign Ministry proposing that this unusual opportunity be used to further anti-Anglo-American propaganda.[23] Two days later, the Japanese government decided that his suggestion would be the best method for launching a vehement propaganda offensive against the British and American invasion of Asia and decided to set up a special week called "A Week to Attack Anglo-American Imperialism" to condemn the hypocrisies contained in the Allied espousal of democracy and freedom.[24]

At the same time, Japan manipulated its puppet government in Nanjing to denounce the "hypocritical democracy and equality" of the Allied Powers. The anti-Allied propaganda was highlighted in late August in the Japanese occupied areas. On August 29, 1942, on the 100th anniversary of the ratification of the Nanjing Treaty, the first treaty of Anglo-American imperialism in East Asia, the Wang Jing-wei government in Nanjing convened a momentous mass rally. At the rally, Wang Jing-wei condemned the unequal treaty forced upon the Chinese by the British and American imperialists as well as American racial discrimination legislation against the Chinese people. He also appealed to the Chinese to unite with the Japanese, to "drive away all the American and British imperialists from Asia" in order to "vitalize East Asia."[25] With a high spirit of Chinese nationalist consciousness, a tremendous "Down with Anglo-American Imperialism" movement prevailed in the Japanese occupied areas.

ⅲ. Chinese Exclusion and American Response

After America's entry into the war, legal discrimination against the Chinese was brought to the attention of American public, in particular to the concern of pro-China intellectuals. Pearl S. Buck, for example, America's first woman Nobel Prize winner, who spent most of her life in China and was known as the most influential Westerner to write about China since Marco Polo,[26] emerged as one of the strongest wartime defenders of freedom and equality for the Chinese. For instance, on March 14, 1942, addressing for the celebration of India-China Friendship Day in New York, Buck urged her audience that "our democracy has been marred by imperialism" because "we are only partial democracy" and American freedom was not for "all the principle of human government."[27]

On May 18, 1942, an article entitled "Exclusion and Extraterritoriality" was published in *Contemporary China*. The author denounced the "white supremacy" of American immigration laws and the perniciousness of the extraterritorial system in China, and demanded that "the era of the unjust system" applied to the Chinese must "come to an end."[28] Three month later, in order to silence Japanese propaganda, another article came out, entitled "This Is No Racial War," which called for freedom and equality to be given to "all the oppressed races and nations."[29]

On the other hand, Chinese demands for equality emerged. Typical of these voices was Soong May-ling, well-known as Madame Chiang Kai-shek. On April 23, 1942, Madame Chiang Kai-shek issued a statement in the *New York Times* condemning the evils of the extraterritorial rights of the Western Powers in China and stated that "the Westerners must change their attitudes towards China" and "give Chinese real freedom which is based on principles of equality."[30]

In response to public opinion, on August 13, Roger S. Green, a former U.S. diplomat in China and a prominent wartime pro-China lobbyist, wrote to his friend Stanley Hornbeck to ask the State Department to concern itself with this issue, since it would "help to convince some doubters in Asia that we really do mean that the Atlantic Charter shall apply to the Far East as much as Europe."[31]

In addition, on August 17, Senator Elbert D. Thomas, a member of the Senate Committee on Foreign Relations, urged Congress to abolish the unequal treaties with China as soon as possible. He addressed the Senate:

As a war measure, the United States and Great Britain should say to China that they renounce their extraterritorial rights. I cannot conceive why we should wait until peace comes to negotiate an extraterritorial agreement with China. When the Japanese have rushed us, and the Chinese with us, as the British, and practically all the extraterritorial law, out of China at the present time.... I know of no better time to renounce our rights than on August 29, 1942, 100 years after the imposition of the Opium War Treaty.[32]

In light of increased popular sentiment in favor of action toward abolition, the State Department decided to consider the extraterritoriality issue. Since Secretary of State Cordell Hull insisted on "a common interest" among the Allies, he suggested cooperating with Britain. On August 27, Hull discussed with British Ambassador in Washington, Viscount Halifax possible abrogation of extraterritoriality.[33] On September 5, Hull urged the American ambassador in London, John G. Winant to convince the British government to take an affirmative step in the matter of abolition.[34] Since Britain enjoyed more privileges than any other power in China after the Opium War, particularly its interests in Hong Kong, the British government was not willing to relinquish its special rights. Finally, the American and British governments conceded to conclude brief treaties with China, which would provide for abolition of extraterritorial rights in China.

During the negotiating process, the United States insisted that this abolition strategy would accomplish the following three principle objectives. First, it would have psychological and political benefits to the cause of the Allied Powers, which would be of concrete assistance to China and strengthen the determination of the Chinese war effort. Second, it would eliminate an existing anomaly in relations with China. Third, it would enable the United States to earn Chinese trust in wartime and postwar world. Subsequently, the British government agreed to abolish its extraterritorial rights in China. Both of the governments decided to inform the Chinese government on October 10, the Independence Day of the Republic of China, that they would abolish their extraterritorial and related rights in China and announced in the press in the two countries to reinforce the propaganda effect.[35]

Immediately, the action of the Allied Powers won great enthusiasm from the Chinese government. On October 10, 1942, President Roosevelt sent a "special gift" to China in the form of his statement to Chiang Kai-shek that the United States had decided to rescind the unequal treaties.[36] Chiang, greatly moved by this unexpected action, sent a telegram to Roosevelt: "Unquestionably, it will boost morale of our Chinese people to fight against aggression bravely." He added, "Any other actions cannot compare with the abolition of the unequal treaties."[37] On the same day, Chiang addressed in the radio, "To abolish the unequal treaties with the Powers is not an important milestone in the history of the revival of the Chinese nation, but also a brilliant lighthouse to guide human progress on the road toward freedom and equality for all mankind."[38] The American ambassador, Clarence Gauss, reported to the State Department on Chinese enthusiasm for the abolition and stated that this Anglo-American policy would be "a big blow to Japanese propaganda efforts."[39]

Nevertheless, China's equality with the United States in international law, as indicated by the relinquishment of the unequal treaties, did not suggest any fundamental sense of racial equality and silence the Japanese propagandists. A few days after the ratification of the new treaty between China and the United States on January 11, 1943, Cheng Gong-bo, Minister of Justice in the Wang puppet regime, issued a statement in Japanese media denouncing the evils of racial discrimination against the Chinese and African Americans. Minister Cheng declared that the Chinese were ready to "share hardship" with Japan in this war because Chinese and Japanese were the same race fighting for the same cause.[40]

Figure 19: The Achilles Heel of the Allied Powers - Racism

The use of graphic arts in promoting political and social message was a significant part at wartime propaganda campaign. This cartoon was published in the Japanese military occupied areas in China. Wang Jing-wei regime used racial issue to encourage Chinese people to fight the war for equality. It satirizes American racial segregation policy by saying that African Americans had never been treated equally in American society. Many African Americans eagerly volunteered to join the Allied cause following America's entry into the war. There were 125,000 African Americans who fought overseas during World War II, but U.S. armed forces remained segregated. African

Americans were considered second class citizens and suffered a heavy racial segregation in the armed forces.

(Source: *Zhongshan Ribao,* December 20, 1942)

Immediately following the attack on Pearl Harbor, the military leaders of Japan turned their sight to the China battlefield. The Japanese forces engaged in psychological warfare in attempts to discourage Chiang Kai-shek's troops and won over the Chinese people. In addition, Japanese propagandists distributed leaflets widely in China attacking the double standards of the Allied democracies. A typical Japanese one read:

At present the U.S. government has improved the treaties with China. You might think that the overseas Chinese in the U.S. have received good treatment due to the relations of allies. This sweet-worded but ugly-faced U.S. is doing this for the face of Chunking (Chongqing).... But facts are contrary. For instance, the U.S. drafted innumerable single Chinese and put them in the army. Talking about singles, the Chinese in the U.S. had to leave their wives in China, because of the Immigration Laws, are classified as singles. Thus they denied their wives in China from entering America. This is the attitude of the U.S. toward Allied peoples who are fighting under the same common principle. Our Japan has never badly treated the Chinese that are in Japan and have never forced the Chinese into army. The difference between the inhuman nature of the Americans and the nature of our Japanese could be seen by facts.[41]

During World War II, leaflets were dropped widely by Japanese airplanes on the Chinese mainland and Southeastern Asian countries, using them to surrenders as the Japanese would be much better than the white Europeans and Americans because of their racial discrimination laws against the Asian peoples. Another typical leaflet stated:

America is China's ally. Americans say they love and admire the Chinese. But can you go to America, can you become citizens? No, Americans do not want you. They just want you to fight. Their Exclusion Act names you and says you are unfit for American citizenship.... There will be no such discrimination against you in the Greater East Asia Co-prosperity Sphere.[42]

Japanese propaganda, such as this, directed at America's anti-Chinese immigration laws, attempted to appeal to Asian peoples by emphasizing the American racial discrimination. As the matter of fact, the Japanese propaganda campaign was not only directly toward the United States but also towards Asian countries that they sought to conquer.

In support of Japan's strategy, on June 24, 1943, an editorial entitled "The Hypocritical and Ugly Face of the United States" was published in *Zhonghua Ribao*, an official newspaper controlled by the Wang Jing-wei's puppet regime. Its author condemned the hypocrisy of American democracy and proclaimed that "if the American government does not repeal the discriminatory laws against the Chinese, Asian people have no real equality." Subsequently, it appealed to "all Asians to unite together to drive away American and British imperialists from Asia in order to establish a prosperous Asia for the Asian peoples."[43]

Figure 20: "Roosevelt: The Chinese Are More Dangerous Than the Negroes"

This cartoon denounced America's discriminatory laws against the Chinese. Over 16,000 Chinese-Americans served in the United States Army during World War II. However, Chinese-American soldiers who volunteered to join the army forces began to fight against Roosevelt's government because of their hatred of the anti-Chinese laws which prohibited their wives to enter American shores.

(Source: *Zhongshan Ribao*, December 24, 1942)

Meanwhile, while visiting Japan in June, 1943, U. B. Lwin, Burma's Minister of Education, addressed in Tokyo, supporting the concept of "Asia for the Asiatics." He stated that Burma saw itself as "an integral part of Asia." "We are Orientals," he added, "and [the] Japanese are also the Orientals. As Orientals, we are proud to see the Japanese achieving victory unprecedented in history. Therefore, we in Burma should do our best for the ultimate victory of Japan in this war."[44]

America's racially discriminatory laws were thus a vital resource for Japan in its campaign of "Asia for the Asiatics." It should be borne in mind, however, just how little the Japanese new ideal order of "the Greater East Asia Co-Prosperity" was itself based upon equality. In January 1941, the Japanese government unequivocally declared that the foundation for establishing the new order was based on the "Yamato people."[45] On January 16, 1942, Japanese Prime Minister Tojo Hideki reiterated in the Imperial Diet the principle that within the new order only the Japanese could be the "Meishu" (master) in "the Greater East Asia Co-Prosperity Sphere."[46]

Figure 21: "Five Races Under One Union"

The Japanese propaganda campaign was not only directly toward the United States but also towards whom they sought to conquer in Asia. This poster widely distributed in Japan's military occupied area in northeast China, "Manchukuo" during the wartime. It attempted to show Japan's ideal to establish a new order of racial harmony. "With the cooperation of Japan, China and Manchukuo, the world can be peaceful," it propagated. (Source: http://en.wikipedia.org.)

Note

---

[1] Brian Niiya, ed., *Japanese American History* (Los Angeles: The Japanese American National Museum, Facts on File, Inc., 1996), p.16.

[2] *The San Francisco Chronicle*, December 8, 1941.

[3] For the Japanese American internment in World War II, see Richard Reeves, *Infamy: The Shocking Story of the Japanese American Internment in World War II* (New York: Henry Hold and Co., 2015).

[4] Zhang Yu-fa, ed., *Zhongguo xiandaishi lunji* [Selected Works on Modern Chinese History] Vol.9, (Taibei, 1982), p.383.

[5] U.S. Department of State, *Papers Relating to the Foreign Relations of the United States*, 1942 (Britain), p.1. (Hereafter cited as *FRUS*).

[6] U.S. Department of State, *Bulletin*, Vol.6, January 3, 1942.

[7] *FRUS*, 1942 (China), p.443.

[8] U.S. House of Representatives, *Hearings before the Committee on Immigration and Naturalization, Repeal of the Chinese Exclusion Acts*, 78th Congress., 1st Session, May and June 1943, p.249. (Hereafter cited as House *Hearings*).

[9] Iriye Akira, *Power and Culture*, p.142.

[10] U.S. Department of State, *Bulletin*, May 2, 1942, p.381.

[11] Iriye Akira, *Power and Culture,* pp.53-54.

[12] *FRUS*, 1942 (China), p.186.

[13] For the relinquishment of extraterritorial rights in China, see Xiaohua Ma, "The Invisible War between the United States and Japan: A Study of the

Abolition of Extraterritoriality in 1943," *The Journal of American and Canadian Studies*, Vol.15, 1997, pp.93-112.

[14] *Asahi Shimbun*, December 13, 1941.

[15] *Toa Kaihou* [Emancipation of East Asia], February 1942, p.62.

[16] "Open Letters to Asian Peoples," *Asahi Shimbun*, June 24-30, 1942.

[17] *Asahi Shimbun*, June 25 1942.

[18] Daitoa senso kankei yikken: Senden no ken [Files Relating to the Greater East Asia War: Issues of Propaganda], January 1943, Foreign Ministry of Japan,Tokyo.

[19] *FRONT*, Vol.5-6, 1943.

[20] *Ibid.*, pp.22-23.

[21] *The New York Times*, May 31, 1942.

[22] U.S. State Department, *Bulletin*, May 2, 1942, p.381.

[23] Shigemitsu Mamoru to Foreign Ministry, August 17, 1942, Daitoa senso kankei ikken: Kakkoku no taido - chuka minkoku (kokumin seifu) [Files Relating to the Greater East Asia War: The Attitudes of the Governments - The Chinese National Government], Foreign Ministry of Japan, Tokyo.

[24] *Ibid.*

[25] *Zhonghua Ribao* [China Daily], August 29, 1942.

[26] Peter Conn, *Pearl Buck: A Cultural Biography* (New York: Cambridge University Press, 1996).

[27] Pearl S. Buck, "Freedom for All", addressed at the Waldorf-Astoria, New York, March 14, 1942, and reprinted in *Asia Magazine,* May 1942.

[28] "Exclusion and Extraterritoriality," *Contemporary China,* May 18, 1942,

pp.1-4.

[29] "This Is No Racial War," *ibid.*, August 10, 1942, pp.2-4.

[30] *The New York Times*, April 23, 1942.

[31] Roger S. Greene to Stanley Hornbeck on August 13, 1943, Roger S. Greene Papers, Houghton Library, Harvard University.

For research on Roger S. Greene's connection with China, see Warren I. Cohen, *The Chinese Connection: Roger S. Greene, Thomas W. Lamont, George E. Sokolsky and American-East Asian Relations* (New York: Columbia University Press, 1978).

[32] U.S. Congress, *Congressional Record*, 77th Congress, 2nd Session, Vol.LXXXVIII, pp.6856-6857.

[33] Secretary of State (Hull) to the Ambassador Halifax in the United States, August 27, 1942, *USFR*, 1942, pp.282-286.

[34] Telegram of the Secretary of State Hull to the Ambassador in the United Kingdom (Winant), September 5, 1942, *FRUS*, 1942, pp.287-288.

[35] *Ibid*, p.287.

[36] Zhongguo Guomingdang Zhongyang Weiyuanhui Danshi Weiyuanhui (Qing Xiao-yi, chief editor), ed., *Zhonghuaminngguo Zhongyao Shiliao Chubian: Duiri Kangzhan Shiqi* [Important Historical Documents of the Republic of China: During the Period of the Anti-Japanese War], Part 3, Vol.3, (Taiwan: Central Book Publishing Co., 1981), p.712. (Hereafter cited as *ZZSC*)

[37] *ZZSC*, p.713; and Chiang Kai-shek, *China's Destiny* (New York: Macmillan, 1947), p.151.

[38] Chiang Kai-shek, *China's Destiny*, p.151.

[39] Telegram of the Ambassador in China (Gauss) to the Secretary of State (Hull), October 12, 1942, *FRUS*, 1942, pp.311-312.

[40] *Chuo Koron*, January 1943, pp.123-125.

[41] Committee on Immigration and Naturalization, House of Representatives, 78th Congress, *Samples of Japanese-Controlled Radio Comments on America's Exclusion Act* (confidential print), 1943, p.2. National Archives, Washington D.C.

[42] This leaflet is recorded in U.S. Congress, *Congressional Record*, 78th Congress, 1st Session, Vol.89, Part 11, p.3127.

[43] *Zhonghua Ribao*, June 24, 1943.

[44] *The Public Opinion*, Summer 1943, pp.200-201.

[45] *Asahi Shimbun*, January 28, 1941.

[46] Foreign Ministry of Japan, ed., *Nippon gaiko bunsho narabini shuyo bunsho* [Important Documents on the Foreign Relations of Japan] (Tokyo, 1969), pp.576-578.

IV. Interaction of America's Foreign Policy and Immigration Policy

Japan's use of the Chinese Exclusion Acts to fight a propaganda war against the Allies embarrassed the United States, since China was its most populous ally in Asia. Furthermore, the assumption of "white superiority" impeded America's influence on Asian countries and domination of the ideological battlefront of the Pacific War. Having been battered by a vehement offensive from Japan's propaganda guns, the United States decided to eliminate the "unfortunate barrier" on the ideological battlefield.

i. American View of China: Soong May-ling's U.S. Tour

The outbreak of the Pacific War in 1941 altered America's traditional attitude towards China, although there had been a wholly sympathetic view of China and its people among the American public before the Pacific War broke out. This pro-China sentiment originated before Japan's attack at Pearl Harbor and could be traced to a deeper American sense of attachment to the Chinese. When Japan invaded China on July 7, 1937, Americans showed great sympathy for the Chinese. Public opinions polls during the Sino-Japanese War demonstrated popular support for the Chinese. According to a Gallup Poll carried out in August 1937, 43% of Americans sympathized with the Chinese, and the favorable rate increased to 74% in 1939.[1]

After the Pearl Harbor attack, American sympathy for the Chinese grew even stronger, for the Chinese were a people who had long been bravely fighting against Japanese aggressors. Two days after the attack, an editorial appearing in the *New York Times* argued that if the United States cooperated with China, "a loyal ally with…inexhaustible manpower," it would have "the key to the strategy of the Pacific."[2] In April 1942, another editorial entitled "China's Splendid Fight" came out in the *New Republic*, in which the author insisted that China, "by virtue of her dogged struggle for independence" could help the United States "immeasurably in winning the war quickly."[3]

Meanwhile Paul G. Hoffman, national chairman of United China Relief, called for the American public to give more aid to China. "This country needs China as much as China needs us in the conflict with Japan," he asserted, "investment in Chinese morale as a vital move will help us to win this war and win it quickly."[4] Thus, the heroic and continuous Chinese struggle against Japanese aggression won high praise from the American public.

On the other hand, the American press and other media fostered the impression that the Chinese under the leadership of Chiang Kai-shek and his American-educated wife Soong May-ling were fighting valiantly against Japanese aggression. American pro-China sentiment culminated in a powerful wartime wave stimulated by Mme. Chiang Kai-shek's national tour to the United States in 1943. Soong May-ling arrived in the United States on November 27, 1942, supposedly for medical treatment, but stayed on until May 1943. To represent her husband and Nationalist China, she made her visit into a national campaign tour.

Early in February, Madame Chiang visited the White House as the special guest of Eleanor and Franklin D. Roosevelt and was invited to address both houses of Congress on February 18, 1943. During her address, Mme. Chiang said "the 160 years of traditional friendship between our two countries….which has never been marred by misunderstandings, is unsurpassed in the annals of the world." She emphasized that "Americans as well as Chinese, who are privileged to help make a better world for ourselves and for posterity must have vision so that peace should not be punitive in spirit and should not be provincial or nationalistic or even continental in concept, but universal in scope and humanitarian in action." [5] Furthermore, Mme. Chiang affirmed Chinese-American solidarity and pleaded for increased military aid from the United States.

While showing China's strong desire for justice and freedom in her address, Mme. Chiang Kai-shek expressed Chinese determination to cooperate with the United States to construct a peaceful and democratic world, which "must be based on justice, coexistence, cooperation, and mutual respect."[6] Then Mme. Chiang turned to her own experience in the United States and confessed that "coming here today I fell that I am also coming home." And it was her home, but also home for her nation, and thus for the mankind. She added:

I believe, however, that it is not only I whom am coming home, I feel that if Chinese people could speak to you in your own tongue, or if you could understand our tongue, they would tell you that basically and fundamentally we were fighting for the same cause, that we have identity of ideals, that the Four Freedoms which your President proclaimed to the world resound throughout our vast land as the gong of freedom, the gong of the freedom of the United Nations, and the death-knell of the aggressors....

I assure you that our people are willing and eager to cooperate with you in the realization of these ideals, because we want to see it that they do not echo as empty phrases but become realities, for ourselves, for our children's children, and for all mankind.[7]

The contents of Mme. Chiang's speech were most beautifully laid out in terms of the English language. Her spoke English was so fluent that it was virtually impossible to tell her Chinese origin. The important message that Mme. Chiang attempted to send was that there was no difference between American and Chinese values. Most importantly, Mme. Chiang directly told Americans that China's war against Japan was no longer China's own war: it was a war of American values against Fascist aggressors. In sum, it was a war for the peace of the world, and it was a war for the mankind.

Figure 22: Soong May-ling in the U.S. Congress

(Source: Franklin D. Roosevelt Library).

The speech was a triumph. The senators and representatives were "captivated and amazed" by this "graceful, charming and intelligent" Chinese First Lady. Mme. Chiang's address was rated as "one of the most impressive and effective speeches" ever made in

Congress.[8] Mme. Chiang spoke English with a strong American accent and was a staunch Christian. All this convinced Americans that China was no longer a fractured country, but America's heroic ally in Asia. From American perspective, Mme. Chiang's achievement was a celebration of American values. Thus, to help China, was like helping Americans themselves to build a new world for freedom and democracy.

Soong May-ling was the first woman to address both houses in the U.S. Congress.[9] Her speech about the importance of China in the war encouraged Americans to send more weapons and financial support to her husband's Nationalist China.

Having heard Madame Chiang's speech, American poet Pliny A. Wiley paid a special tribune to this "special envoy" from China:

Mme. Chiang Kai-shek

She spoke and all our Congress heard
　This voice from China's ancient land
While truth and logic graced her every word
　Of flawless English all could understand.

She spoke and Washington's great power
　Inclined to hear and answer to her call;
Inclined to help this woman of the hour
　Whose eloquence and diction had won her hearers all.

She spoke and our Republic gave
  Her rapt attention to the every end
And vowed to send across Pacific's wave
  All aid and comfort to our Chinese friend.

She spoke and mankind understood,
  Heedless of color, race, or creed,
Her plea for world-wide brotherhood,
  Humanity was crying in its need.[10]

Thus, Soong May-ling, in American eyes, was much more than the wife of the Chinese leader. In American eyes, she had become the symbol of Chinese resistance: brave, intelligent, charming, articulate, and to top it all, elegant.

Two weeks later, Madame Chiang visited New York City and continued to campaign the United States for increased military support. In her speech at Madison Square Garden on March 3, 1943, Madame Chiang said:

All nations, great and small, must have equal opportunity of development. Those who are stronger and more advanced should consider their strength as a trust to be used to help the weaker nations to fit themselves for full-government and not to exploit them. Exploitation is spiritually as degrading to the exploiters as to the exploited.[11]

While showing China's strong desire for justice and equality in the international affairs, Madame Chiang expressed deep Chinese desire to cooperate with the United States to build a peaceful world in the postwar era. "No matter what we have undergone and suffered," she added, "we must try to forgive those who injured us and remember only the lesson gained thereby."[12]

Throughout spring of 1943, Madame Chiang traveled around the United States, from Washington D.C. to New York to Boston to Chicago to San Francisco to Los Angeles, pumping up American concerns for Nationalist China at every stop and arousing American enthusiasm for China. No matter wherever she traveled, Madame Chiang tried every effort to arouse the American public for more military support to China, which was under the leadership of her Christian husband.

In the American press and media, for example, Henry R. Luce's *Time* and *Life*, Madame Chiang was regarded as not only "the voice of Free China," but also as "the voice of Asia." Meantime, her husband, Chiang Kai-shek, was depicted as building a "strong" and "democratic" China, which would remain America's closest Asian ally in the postwar era. As an editorial in the *Washington Post* pointed out, "in American eyes Free China has become a great power with the title to determine the next world polity gained from its outstanding services in the extinction of world tyranny."[13] However, how could China become a "Great Power" while the Chinese were still excluded by American legislation?

81

Figure 23: Chinese-Americans Welcome Mme. Chiang Kai-shek

In late March, 1943, Soong May-ling visited Los Angeles and made a speech in Los Angeles' Chinatown on March 31, 1943. Thousands of Chinese Americans came to welcome her on the street.

(Source: *Los Angeles Times*, March 31, 1943)

ii . American Campaign for the Repeal of Chinese Exclusion

After the United States entered the war, legal discrimination against the Chinese was brought to the forefront of American public awareness. In February 1942, Charles N. Spinks, a specialist on East

Asian relations, wrote an article, "Repeal Chinese Exclusion" in *Asia and the Americas*. He pointed out that the Untied States was now fighting side by side with China, one of its most important allies, to destroy fascism and to build a new world order based on the fundamental principles of freedom, justice and equality for mankind. Nevertheless, he argued, the Untied States was not treating "the Chinese people, our allies, with the justice and equality they deserve."[14]

In addition, other articles referred to the serious effect of Japanese propaganda, which was using Chinese exclusion to "spread rumors" in Asia. They argued that the danger was the more acute since Japan controlled not only "the radio but all forms of communication and social organization throughout Asia." The main arguments of the advocates were that Japanese racial propaganda would not only menace America's interests in East Asia but also would contribute to the quick defeat of the Allied forces in the war, because it focused on the undeniable fact that Chinese were excluded by American immigration laws. In sum, they suggested the government to quickly "end the affront to China" in order to destroy Japan completely and win the war for justice.[15]

The outbreak of the Pacific War altered America's attitude towards the Chinese. Moreover, Madame Chiang's national tour around America in early 1943 demonstrated that China shared the principles of democracy with the United States. In the meantime, equality for all, which was one of the oldest American ideals, now became a new symbol of American democracy and freedom, brought forth again in the process of fighting against fascist aggression and winning the war. Pearl S. Buck, a well-known American Nobel-Prize winner, used every occasion to press her demands for racial equality.

In February 1942, for example, speaking at a literary luncheon, Buck surprised the 1,700 people gathered in New York. "The Japanese weapon of racial propaganda in Asia is beginning to show signs of effectiveness," she told her audience, "prejudice is the most vulnerable term in our American democracy."[16] She indicated in her address that victory in the war demanded the cooperation of peoples regardless of race, color or nation. If Americans did not abandon "white supremacy," the United States would lose the war. "We cannot win this war, " she asserted, "without convincing our colored allies – who are most of our allies – that we are not fighting for ourselves as continuing superior over colored peoples."[17]

A month later, in a radio broadcast, Pearl S. Buck emphasized that the aim of America's war was to "give real freedom and human equality to all people."[18] In order to arouse public concern, Buck toured the country to criticize racial discrimination in American society. While visiting Washington D.C. on June 5, 1942, she made an address to call for terminating discriminatory laws against colored peoples:

Discrimination in our country must go, because until it does, we will not have won the war. We cannot fight for freedom unless we fight for freedom for all. We are not better than fascists if we fight for the freedom of one group and not another, for the benefit of one race and not another, for the aggrandizement of a part and not the betterment of the whole.[19]

Pearl S. Buck wrote numerous articles and books to criticize the racism in the American society. On April 25, 1942, in her letter titled "What Are We Fighting for in the Orient" to *The Christian Science Monitor*, Buck condemned the United States for not treating China as "an equal ally" because the Chinese were discriminated in American immigration laws. "This war is a dozen civil wars, an interracial war," she continued, "If the United States ignored one or suppressed one it would be to end in disaster."[20]

In sum, in a variety of ways, in books, in magazines, in speeches and on the radio, Buck concluded bluntly that discrimination against the Chinese in the United States must "come to an end," because while it existed, "we are fighting on the wrong side on the war. We belong with Hitler."[21] She continued her crusade for total freedom and equality for all people throughout the war. Buck and her second husband, Richard J. Walsh, who was her publisher and chief editor of *Asia and the Americas*, became leading figures in the movement to abolish Chinese exclusion. Under their leadership, a national campaign to repeal the Chinese Exclusion Acts was begun.

On November 10, 1942, Richard Walsh made a speech at the Town Hall Round Table of New York City, urging that the United States repeal the Chinese Exclusion Acts, place Chinese immigration on a quota basis, and make Chinese people eligible for American citizenship.[22] His speech evoked a tremendous reaction. In the spring of 1943, "The Citizens Committee to Repeal Chinese Exclusion and Place Immigration on a Quota Basis" was formed in New York City by a group of notable intellectuals, including Pearl S. Buck, Henry R, Luce, founder of *Time, Life* and *Fortune*, and retired Admiral Harry R. Yarnell. Over 250 persons, representing more than 40 states, joined the Citizens Committee, and hundreds more worked in close cooperation with the members and other organizations. These pro-China intellectuals served as the chief spokespersons in the repeal campaign. Richard J. Walsh, chairman of the Citizens Committee, appealed to the members in May 1943, "Last year we celebrated Double Ten [October 10, China's Independence Day] by announcing the end of extraterritoriality....This year let Double Ten resound with the news that we have repealed the exclusion laws."[23]

In the meantime, the Citizens Committee published a pamphlet – *Our Chinese Wall* – to arouse public interest. Over 30,000 copies were distributed to libraries, universities, and religious, social and labor organizations. The Citizens Committee began to influence public opinion in favor of repealing the Chinese Exclusion Acts. The strategy of the Citizens Committee was to stress the military necessity of counteracting the Japanese propaganda that was disturbing amicable U.S. relations with China.[24]

The first meeting was held on May 25, 1943 and three objectives were adopted: repeal of the Chinese exclusion acts, eligibility of Chinese for naturalization, and quota basis for Chinese. Meantime, three strategic decisions emerged from this meeting. The first was to concentrate on Chinese exclusion repeal rather than elimination of the ban against all Asian immigration. The basis for this decision was the conviction that, "because of our present close ties with China, it might be possible to put through repeal of Chinese exclusion whereas an attempt to repeal all oriental exclusion laws would almost surely at that time end in defeat." The second was to reject all the bills previously introduced and to stress the three objectives of the Citizens' Committee in every way and through every channel possible. The third policy was to limit membership on the Committee to United States citizens, not to discouraging Chinese from working for repeal, but "to impress Congress with the fact that Americans were demanding the repeal of the antiquated exclusion laws."[25]

Under this strategy, the press, radio and other media channels for the repeal movement were utilized throughout the whole country. Commentators, Round Tables in New York, convention addresses, and local and national radio stations carried many types of programs on behalf of repeal. Congressman Walter H. Judd, a former medical missionary in China for over 12 years, served one of the most active and important spokesmen for the repeal campaign. On September 2, 1943, Judd addressed in Town Meeting of Air, "We must do two things," he said, "We must get more material help to China – more gun, planes, medicines, munitions – and we must get more political help, more to justify and strengthen China's confidence in us." He insisted that "the most dramatic and helpful thing imaginable would be for us to put the Chinese on the same quota basis as our other

Allies, and thereby begin treating them as equals now."[26] Pro-China intellectuals and missionaries began to lobby Congress for the repeal of the Chinese Exclusion Acts.

Note

[1] Harold R. Isaacs, *Images of Asia: American Views of China and India* (New York, 1962), p.173.

[2] *The New York Times*, December 9, 1941.

[3] *The New Republic*, April 40, 1942, p.544.

[4] *The New York Times*, April 23, 1942

[5] *Ibid*, February 18, 1943.

[6] U.S. Congress, *Congressional Record*, 78th Congress, 1st Sessesion,Vol.89, Part 9, p.2124.

[7] *Ibid, pp.* 2123-2124.

[8] *Ibid*, Vol.89, Part 9, p.2124.

[9] Victoria Woodhull (September 23, 1838-June 9, 1927) was an American leader of the woman's suffrage movement. Being an activist for women's rights and labor reform, she was invited to address in the Congressional Committee on January 11, 1871. In 1872, Woodhull became the first female candidate for President of the United States. For detail, see "The First Woman to Address a Congressional Committee." http://history.house.gov/Historical-Highlights/1851-1900/The-first-woman-to-address-a-congressional-committee/.

[10] U.S. Congress, *Congressional Record*, 78th Congress, 1st Session, Vol.89, Part 1, p.819.

[11] *The New York Times*, March 3, 1943.

[12] *Ibid.*

[13] *Washington Post*, February 18, 1943.

[14] Charles Nelson Spinks, "Repeal Chinese Exclusion," *Asia and the Americas*, February 1942, p.92.

[15] Richard J. Walsh, "Freedom and Equality for All," *Asia*, May 1942, pp.258-259; "Our Great War against the Chinese," *The New Republic*, November 23, 1942, pp.671-672; "Repeal Chinese Exclusion Now," *Asia and the Americas*, January 1943, p.4; Eliot Janeway, "Fighting a White Man's War," *Asia and the Americas,* January 1943, pp.4-5; Richard J. Walsh, "Repeal Exclusion Laws Now," *Asia and the Americas*, June 1943, pp.322-323; Quintus Quest, "Drop the Asiatic Color Bar!" *Christian Century*, February 1943, pp.191-192; Y. C. Shen, "High Time to Repeal Anti-Chinese Laws," *Chinese Mind,* June 1943, pp.1-2; Bruno Lasker, "End Exclusion Now," *The New Republic*, May 1943, pp.698-699; and "Our Humiliation – Not Theirs," *Common Ground*, Autumn 1943, pp.71-76.

[16] Pearl S. Buck, "Tinder for Tomorrow," delivered at the Book & Author Luncheon, Astor Hotel, New York, February 10, 1942, reprinted in *Asia*, March 1942, pp.153-155.

[17] *Ibid*.

[18] Pearl S. Buck, "What Are We Fighting for in the Orient?" delivered in Town Meeting of the Air in Town Hall, New York, March 26, 1942, reprinted in *The Christian Science Monitor,* April 25, 1942.

[19] Pear S. Buck addressed at Howard University, Washington, June 5, 1942, printed in Pearl S. Buck, *What America Means to Me* (New York: John Day Co., 1942), p.27.

[20] The *Christian Science Monitor*, April 25, 1942.

[21] Pearl S. Buck, "Freedom for All," *Asia*, May 1942, pp.324-326.
For detail of Pearl S. Buck's crusade in wartime for freedom and equality,
see Pearl S. Buck, *American Unity and Asia* (New York: John Day Co.,
1942.) and *What America Means to Me* (New York: John Day Co., 1943).

[22] Richard J. Walsh, "Our Great Wall against the Chinese," *The New
Republic*, November 23, 1942, pp.671-672.

[23] Richard J. Walsh's letter to all members, Records of the Citizens
Committee to Repeal Chinese Exclusion and Place Immigration on a Quota
Basis, New York Public Library, New York. (Hereafter cited as Records of
the Citizens Committee)

[24] Richard J. Walsh's letter to all members, *ibid.* Records of the Citizens
Committee.

[25] Report, May 25, 1943, Records of the American Labor Conference on
International Affairs: Files of Citizens Committee to Repeal Chinese
Exclusion and Place Immigration on a Quota Basis, Tamiment Institute
Library, New York University, New York.

[26] Walter H. Judd, "Should we repeal the Chinese Exclusion laws now?"
addressed at Town Meeting of the Air, September 2, 1943, Papers of Walter
H. Judd, Hoover Institution, Stanford University.

V. China in America's New World Order

ⅰ. The Strategy of the State Department

When, with the outbreak of the Pacific War on February 17, 1942, the Japanese propaganda guns also opened fire, an American missionary informed the State Department that the United States should be seriously concerned about Chinese exclusion, because it had both "propagandic and politic value" in the war fighting against Japan's "Greater East Asia War to liberate Asia."[1] Although the State Department realized the issue, it had no intention to solve it, since immigration issue was "regulated strictly by statutes, the enactment or repeal of which falls within the province of the Congress."[2] Therefore, the State Department avoided the "intricate and controversial issue" that would involve "extensive revision of our immigration laws."[3]

On April 6, 1942, Warren A. Seavey, a well-known professor at Harvard Law School, advised the State Department to terminate the injustice towards the Chinese and abandon the anti-Chinese laws immediately, on the grounds that China had succeeded in "holding [back] the Japanese and in aiding India" in the war.[4] The State Department, however, held to the opinion that the government could not proceed with this issue as the United States was at war.[5] The implication was that the Chinese immigration issue should be taken up only after the war.

Nevertheless, Japanese propaganda, which used Chinese

92

exclusion to promote its campaign of "Asia for the Asiatics," continued to bolster Japanese morale in Asia. Especially, as some intellectuals warned the State Department, if the United States lost China's goodwill through continuing discriminating against the Chinese people, it would risk another war in which white supremacy might be ferociously challenged by Asians in general. Therefore, they requested the repeal of the Chinese Exclusion Acts in order to "prevent a third war of white versus colored races."[6]

Figure 24: "The Hypocrisy of American Immigration Laws"

The literature of the time affected how people viewed the war and their enemy, but the visual art created in the wartime drew attention more easily and drew a large audience simply by its nature. This cartoon titled "American Immigration Policy Is Subtle in the Hypocrisy" directly sent the message that American immigration laws were discriminatory against the Chinese people.

(Source: *The Times Weekly*, July 5, 1943)

Before the war, Chinese exclusion was an untouchable cornerstone of American immigration and naturalization policy. A combination of circumstances, however, made the eventual passage of repeal easy. Over the course of 1942, with the Japanese propagandists repeatedly calling on Asians to "drive away all Americans, Britons, and he Dutchmen from Asia," and "let Asia be for the Asiatics," the State Department became concerned about this "psychological" issue which was perceived to be impeding America's domination of Asia.

On June 17, 1942, Maxwell M. Hamilton, Chief of the Division of Far Eastern Affairs in the State Department, pointed out that the Japanese, by pursuing a psychological campaign of "Asia for the Asiatics" and "the colored races of the world united under Japanese leadership against the white races" could achieve the victory in Asia. Having analyzed China's war potential, he indicated that if China collapsed, it would contribute immeasurably to the Axis' psychological offensive, and would "greatly bolster morale in Japan and increase the effectiveness and appeal of Japan's psychological warfare."[7] Subsequently, Hamilton pointed out that China, as the largest Oriental power, could supply the "decisive factor in the psychological warfare against Japan." Secondly, he asserted that China, through its war against Japan, could "dampen moral in Japan itself by her stubborn refusal to accept Japan's program of 'Asia for the Asiatics." As for the role of China's resistance in the war, he concluded that the "psychological factor" should not be ignored in America's war strategy.[8]

For the United States, the importance of China during the wartime was a matter of political propaganda, as well as of political and military strategy. The propaganda had two main goals: first, to strengthen Chinese morale and defeat the Japanese campaign of "Asia for the Asiatics;" second, to meet America's desire to establish a new world order in Asia, which was oriented toward Western democracy instead of Japan's "Greater East Asia Co-Prosperity Sphere." On February 27, 1943, Hamilton directly declared that China's continued involvement in the war on the side of the United States was "the best insurance that the present war not become a race war."[9] In particular, he emphasized that China's role in the war effort was not only "extremely important for the present but for the long future as well."[10] Therefore, it became necessary as part of the propaganda war for the United States to repeal the Chinese Exclusion Acts.

Moreover, Assistant Secretary of State Breckingridge Long pointed out that the "psychological factor" was indispensable in America's relations with China, also with other non-white countries. "More and more, the psychological factor is going to be one of the determining factors in relationships between this country and China,"

95

he insisted, "it may become that in relationships between the Anglo-Saxon peoples and most of the peoples of Asia- even including Russia- and of Africa."[11] Therefore, it became necessary, as part of the propaganda war, for the United States to repeal the Chinese Exclusion Acts.

Figure 25: "We Salute to the Chinese Republic"

This poster was used for American China Aid Campaign in 1942. It says, "China - the First of our allies to fight Japan, China - in spite of war, struggling victoriously toward Democracy as we did 150 years ago."

(Source: Franklin D. Roosevelt Library)

To the State Department, the repeal of Chinese exclusion involved both immediate questions of war strategy and long-term considerations of postwar policy. Subsequently the United States decided to eliminate the "possible obstacle" between the two nations, when Chinese Foreign Minister T. V. Soong requested the repeal of discriminatory laws against the Chinese in March 1943 as the Chinese were "eager for recognition" and "equality."[12]

Meanwhile, the national tour of Madame Chiang aroused a wave of enthusiasm and reinforced American good feeling to China. On February 17, 1943, when Madame Chiang visited the Capital Hill, Congressman Martin J. Kennedy (Democrat, New York) seized "the auspicious occasion" to introduce a bill to grant the Chinese rights to entry into the United States and rights of citizenship.[13] Kennedy's bill was the first bill requesting a repeal of the Chinese exclusion since the acts were enacted in Congress in 1882. Meanwhile, Kennedy sent a letter to Madame Chiang on the same day. "A people which have shared with us the common danger, and will share with us the eventual victory," he wrote, "a people which have earned our friendship, our gratitude, and our respect, have by the same token surely earned our franchise."[14] Subsequently, several bills for repeal of the Chinese Exclusion Acts were introduced in Congress in addition to Kennedy's: Warren G. Magnuson's bill on March 26, and Samuel Dickstein's bill on April 4, 1943.

On May 13, Assistant Secretary of State Breckinridge Long discussed the Chinese issues with House Speaker Sam Rayburn and House Majority Leader John W. McCormack. During the conversation, Long explicitly declared that the State Department would "support a movement to permit the immigration of persons resident in China and born in China to be admitted under the quota." Five days later (May 18), Samuel Dickstein, Chairman of the House Committee on Immigration and Naturalization discussed the issues with Edward J. Shaughnessy, Deputy Administrator of Immigration and Naturalization Service of the Department of Justice, to solve the Chinese immigration issues. The next day, the House Committee on Immigration and Naturalization decided to hold public hearings.[15] On May 19, the first hearing was held to debate the repeal of the Chinese Exclusion Acts.

ⅱ. **China in America's Postwar Strategy**

In May-June of 1943, the House Committee summoned fifty-one witnesses during six hearings. The repeal campaign provoked a strong demonstration of American nativism. The traditional opposition forces, primarily from four sources: labor, veterans' organizations, West Coast interests groups, and traditional "patriotic" societies, took a vigorous stand against Chinese immigration. For example, representatives of the American Coalition, an association representing approximately one hundred patriotic societies expressed a strong, racially motivated, dislike of the Chinese, calling them, for example, "morally the most debased people on the face of the earth."[16] The representatives of the American Federation of Labor argued that the repeal would be "the first step to let the hungry hordes of Europe and Asia pour in to form breadlines in the cities" of the country.[17] In addition, organizations of the Veterans of Foreign Wars strongly opposed a "radical change of immigration laws" from "an economical standpoint."[18]

Popular opposition to Asian immigration also came from various nationalistic groups. Some of these were old organizations which lobbied for passage of the exclusion acts, while others were of a number of new groups. Characteristic of the first type is the labor union associations, for example United American Mechanics had always opposed immigration to the United States. New groups like the National Blue Star Mothers, whose spokesperson, Agnes Waters, appeared before the House Committee on May 26, 1943, opposed repeal of the Chinese exclusion acts because "the Chinese race is a yellow race the white people have to fight." [19] She continued:

I represent millions of American women who are opposed to the breaking down of our immigration laws. I have opposed the breaking down of our immigration laws since 1938 in this committee room; and most especially are we against this particular bill that would repeal the Chinese Exclusion Act. Foreign policy was given to us by our forefathers from the very inception of this Republic to safeguard the American people – I should say the rights for the American people.

While asking the House Committee, "Why flood this country with the yellow race," she repeated Rudyard Kipling's well-known remark on race, "East is east and west is west, and never the twains shall meet." Finally she concluded that "the dangers of invasion from the Asiatics" must be prevented.[20]

In addition, a number of traditional "patriotic" groups strongly opposed the repeal. The representatives of the Society of Mayflower Descendents and the Sons of the American Revolution argued that modification of the immigration laws would cause irreparable injury to the country and, consequently, all such proposals should await consideration until after the war.[21]

However, the pro-repeal force was promoted by influential groups such as the Citizens Committee and missionary organizations. Eventually, forty-two witnesses testified before the Immigration and Naturalization Committee in favor of repealing the Chinese Exclusion Acts. The advocates favored the following three-point program: the repeal of the Chinese Exclusion Acts, the establishment of a quota for Chinese immigrants, and the eligibility of Chinese immigrants for American citizenship. The argument with the widest appeal and greatest weight was that the repeal would help the United States to win the war, and win it quickly.

Pearl S. Buck and Richard J. Walsh testified before the House Committee on May 20, 1943 and insisted that the exclusion acts against the Chinese must be repealed "as a war measure," and that "China must be put on a quota basis with other nations."[22] Buck in her testimony before the House Committee described the Chinese exclusion acts as "a wall of injustice "which unless repealed, would "rise higher and higher between our two peoples." She continued:

> It is more than injustice. It is a denial of our democratic ideals, and this makes the Americans on Chinese soil ashamed. And being ashamed, he is angry at having to bear upon himself and in himself the effects of the injustice and the lack of democracy of his nation. There is a wall between him and the kindly Chinese people. He knows that they are right and he is wrong, and this is hard to bear. I do most earnestly hope, therefore, that as a war measure, if for nothing else, the exclusion acts against the Chinese must be repealed.[23]

The whole repeal campaign reflected the impact of former "China Hands." As already noted, the initial impulse came from Pearl S. Buck, Richard J. Walsh, and Donald Dunham who had been in the U.S. consular service in Hong Kong. Pearl S. Buck and Richard J. Walsh had gained special interest in China through editing *Asia Magazine* and through their close contacts with friends of China. The letter of Richard J. Walsh to more than 4,000 "Friends of China" in August 1943 brought many answers indicating wholehearted support for the repeal.

Figure 26: Pearl S. Buck and the Chinese-Americans

On May 20, 1943, Pearl S. Buck met a group of Chinese-Americans who came to support her before the House Committee on Immigration and Naturalization for the repeal of the Chinese Exclusion Acts.

(Source: University of Pennsylvania Library)

It has been observed that Americans who spent much time in China often return as close friends of the Chinese people, devoted to advancing their interests in the United States. Although they constitute but a minute segment of the total population, their influence on issues relating to China may be considered. Some of them were businessmen in China who shared views of American commercial groups, while others were missionaries naturally ally themselves with the religious organizations from which they came.

When issues involving China arise, they are then in key position to urge action.[24]

Of the forty-two persons testifying for the repeal of the exclusion before the House Committee, nineteen were "Old China Hands." Of these, eight came from missionary backgrounds, seven from business world, two were scholars on Asian issues, and one had been a top naval officer.[25] Among the businessmen, Mansfield Freeman had spent twenty years in China and was president of United States Life Insurance Company, favored repeal, because "trade with China and cooperation with her four hundred million people are going to be very important factors in America's post-war prosperity." He also stressed that "there is no nation which has such potential opportunities in the Far East for the United States."[26] Another businessman was Clarence E. Meyer who had represented the Standard Oil of New York in China for over twenty years stated that the business with China in the post war era was extremely crucial for the development of American economy and "China is going to have tremendous importance for the future" of the country.[27]

Some outstanding witnesses with missionary background, for example, Pearl S. Buck and Walter Judd, however, appeared in other capacities. Testimony of Judd, Representatives from Minnesota, and former missionary doctor in China, filled over twenty-six pages of the House report. Congressman Judd proclaimed in the House Committee that "We can prove by passing this bill to give China an immigration quota on the same basis as other friendly countries that America stands for freedom and equality." He added:

103

China has always had this profound, almost pathetic faith in America. She wants to continue to have it. But such factors as the above have made her begin to doubt….

To make sure that China holds until we can defeat Hitler and bring our full force to bear on Japan, we must do two things: we must get more material help to China, more guns, planes, tanks, gasoline, medicines, supplies, technicians, and so forth; and we must get more necessity of our taking the military offensive in the Pacific as soon as possible; we have not seen how necessary it is that we take and win the political offensive even more quickly…. The most dramatic and helpful thing imaginable would be a removal by Congress of the discrimination laws against the Chinese...

The Chinese all those years have held loyally to us, and they want to continue to hold to us. They will be one of our best and most faithful friends; but you cannot expect to insult a friend indefinitely and then make it all right just by giving him financial or military support, no matter how abundant.

He continued, "The Pacific would be pacific if America has on that side a strong, independent, democratic, friendly China." "There never will be a war between the white and colored races," he concluded "If only we keep the largest and strongest of them, the Chinese, with us."[28]

Admiral H. E. Yarnell, speaking from the perspective of American military strategy, claimed that "the mainland of China the only area from which long-range bombers can reach Japan." This led to the conclusion that Allied success against Japan required the continuance of China in the war. He stressed that "By the repeal of these laws, this means of stirring up hatred of the Western nations will be eliminated." Finally he concluded that it would "have far-reaching effects as a war and a post-war measure" to "put China as an equal nation in every respect with the other three Allied Nations."[29] Therefore, the repeal of the Chinese Exclusion Acts became a new means for the United States to adjust its East Asian policy, especially its China policy.

America's China's policy revealed this impulse in two ways. First, it reflected wartime necessities. Second, it acknowledged the need to address postwar possibilities. When Congressman Warren G. Magnuson introduced the bill to repeal the Chinese Exclusion Acts in Congress in October 1943, he stressed that the repeal of the anti-Chinese discriminatory laws went far beyond America's wartime needs:

This bill goes far above and beyond its present war necessity. If any one position of our foreign policy should be clear in the post-war world it should be this: that we need in the Orient, democracy needs in the Orient, a strong Allied nation, practicing the same principles of democracy that we intend to keep. Without such a strong nation it does not take much intelligence to visualize what might come out of the great cauldron mass of millions of Asiatic peoples. Without the clear leadership of such a democratic Asiatic nation as China, with our help, alliances could form and other Japanese types of destructive empire could arise that would make the present island empire look like a dwarf.[30]

Under Secretary of State Edward R. Stettinius held the same opinion and stressed that the repeal of the anti-Chinese laws should be carried out "in recognition of China's place among the United Nations fighting for democracy and her great future in a democratic world."[31]

What was China's "great future in a democratic world"? For the United States, the most important question had to do with postwar politics. The stabilization of East Asia would require a strong counterweight to the Soviet Union. President Roosevelt outlined this position during British Foreign Minister Anthony Eden, who visited the White House in the fall of 1942. Talking about the role China would play in international politics after the war, Roosevelt told Eden that he believed that "in any serious conflict of policy with Russia, [China] would undoubtedly line up on our side."[32] Therefore, in order for China to be able to take up this position, she must not only emerge from the war as a strong nation with "Great Power" status, but must also be oriented toward the Western Powers and encouraged to practice "the same principles of democracy" as the United States.

On the other hand, China's cooperation was indispensable for the United States in helping to weaken British forces in postwar Asia.

This strategy was expressed clearly in a conversation between U.S. General Joseph Stilwell, the Allied Military Commander in China, and Chiang Kai-shek in the winter of 1943. General Stilwell told Chiang that "the United States was against any form of imperialism, including British," and believed in "a free, strong, democratic China predominant in Asia" after the war.[33] According to the public polls carried out in 1942, Americans believed that China was the most trustful ally after the war (Figure 27).[34] Thus, to the United States, if Japan was to be demilitarized, the emergence of a new China with "Great Power" status would be a prerequisite for the stable and peaceful Asia needed in America's global strategy.

Figure 27: Which Country Can Be Depended upon to Cooperate with the U.S. after the War

1942	Russia	Britain	China
February	38%	76%	80%
May	45%	77%	83%
July	43%	68%	85%
August	51%	72%	86%

Office of War Information, "Report from the Nation, December 7, 1941 – December 7, 1942," President Secretary's File, Box 156, Franklin D. Roosevelt Papers, Franklin D. Roosevelt Library.

What was China's response to the American vision of this new world order in East Asia? During his visit to Chongqing in October 1942, Wendell L. Willkie, President Roosevelt's Special Envoy, told

Chiang that postwar cooperation between the two nations was indispensable to weaken the influence of British imperialism.[35] In response, Chiang explicitly declared China's commitment to cooperation with the United States in the postwar world. [36] Furthermore, in her visit to the United States in early 1943, Madame Chiang declared unequivocally in conversations with President Roosevelt's Special Advisor, Harry L. Hopkins, that China would strongly support the United States in international affairs.[37] This commitment to "support America's proposals once a divergence of views among the United States, Britain, and the Soviet Union occurs," became one of the most important principles for China's role in postwar international politics.[38] Therefore, "practicing the same principles of democracy" and maintaining "pro-Americanism" in China that emerged after the war was an indispensable American political objective.

During the repeal campaign, the State Department worked indirectly for repeal of the Chinese exclusion acts. It considered with Congressional leaders, with Committee members and with the ranking officers of the opposition. In this process Breckinridge Long, Assistance Secretary of State Department responsible for liaison with Congress, was very active. In the spring of 1943, Assistant Secretary Long held conferences with the House Speaker Sam Rayburn, Majority Leader John W. McCormack alone, with majority members of the Immigration Committee of the House to deal with the Chinese issues. When President Roosevelt made a statement to Congress on October 11, at the same time the State Department sent a formal letter supporting the bill to Senator Richard Russell, Chairman of the Senate Immigration Committee, and to the House Speaker Rayburn. In the letters, the State Department pointed out that it was important to promote amicable relations with China and that removal of the discriminatory laws against the Chinese, which had long caused misunderstanding, would serve this end. Extraterritoriality had already been relinquished, it was pointed out, and the exclusion laws should also go. Furthermore, it stressed that the repeal would help nullify Japanese propaganda which impeded U.S. relations with China.[39]

ⅲ. The Congressional Committee: Toward the Final Repeal

The committee in Congress played a fundamental role in determining the course of legislation, particularly because the committee chairman may hold views at variance with those of the dominant party and the party leaders find it difficult to bring bills to a vote which may be opposed by a standing committee. Consequently in the repeal campaign of the Chinese exclusion laws in 1943, the specific attitudes and actions must be taken into account.

The Immigration and Naturalization Committee of the House played a particularly crucial role in the repeal campaign. During his long term as chairman of the House Committee on Immigration and Naturalization, Samuel Dickstein (Democrat, New York) had consistently favored bills liberalizing the immigration law. Born in a traditional Jewish family in Lithuania, he emigrated to the United

States with his parents when he was a little boy. Because of his Jewish immigrant background, he showed great sympathy for European refugees and Chinese immigrants.[40] In the legislative process, he introduced two bills for the repeal of the Chinese exclusion laws. Therefore, Chairman Dickstein's active support was an important asset for the repeal advocates. The unfavorable effects of hostility toward him or his Committee's strategies were offset by the advantages of having as chairman of the Immigration Committee a man who was willing to work for the success of the repeal cause.

The Committee had twenty-one members, eleven of whom were Democrats, and ten Republicans, including its chairman. Among the Democrats, eight came from southern states. On the basis of their remarks during the House Committee hearings, it appears that all three of the northern Democratic members favored the repeal, while of the eight southern members, four definitely opposed. Ed Gossett was the only southern member to state unequivocal support the repeal. Robert Ramspeck's remarks in Committee showed him to be somewhat doubtful, but later in the House debate he committed himself to support the repeal. The attitude of Arthur Winstead and John L. McMillan could not be determined. From this it would appear that the Democratic members were about equally divided pro and con, with two or three doubtful members. The attitudes of the members in the House Immigration and Naturalization Committee are given below:

Figure 28: Attitudes of Members in Immigration and
Naturalization Committee

Attitudes of Members of House Immigration and Naturalization Committee					
Democrats		Attitude	**Republicans**		Attitude
Samuel Dickstein	NY	○○	Noah M. Mason	ILL	○
Arthur Winstead	MISS	△	Edward O. McCowen	OHIO	×
Dan R. McGehee	MISS	△	Carl T. Curtis	NEB	○
Lex Green	FLA	×	Hubert S. Ellis	W. VA	×
John Lesinski	MICH	○○	Lowell Stockman	ORE	○
A. Leonard Allen	LA	×	Bernard W. Kearney	NY	○
Robert Ramspeck	GA	○	William P. Elmer	MO	×
Ed Gossett	TEX	○○	John B. Bennett	MICH	×
Thomas Scanlon	PA	○	Edward H. Rees	KAN	△
O. C. Fisher	TEX	×	Joseph Farrington	HAWAII	○
John L. McMillan	SC	△			
Note: 1) ○○ favorable and introduced repeal bill					
2) × opposed 3) △ indefinite					

(Source: *Congressional Directory*, May 14, 1943, p.202)

The Republican members of the Committee were also divided almost equally on the repeal question. Of the nine voting members, four definitely opposed and four favored, while Edward H. Rees was indefinite. Four Republican members Hubert S. Ellis, Edward O. McCowen, John B. Bennett, and William R. Elmer signed in the minority report opposing the repeal bill. Joseph Farrington of Hawaii testified at the House hearings and supported the repeal. Lowell Stockman was the only member from the West Coast, but he did not participate in the House hearings. Since the Chinese Exclusion Acts were enacted because of the pressure of the West Coast, his attitude may have proved an influential factor. According to a House Committee report, he favored the repeal.[41]

A. Leonard Allen, who strongly opposed the repeal, spoke much more often than the other members, and quite clearly led the opposition. Apart from the Chairman Dickstein, John Lesinski and Gossett were the chief supporters and they even introduced bills for the repeal campaign. At the executive session on June 7, 1943, the majority of the Committee members favored the repeal alone, but opposed the quota. Doubtless a few members of this majority supported repeal as a war measure but considered that the quota would introduce domestic complications which they could not accept.

When the House Committee voted on the Magnuson bill in October, the count eight to four was in favor of the bill. Both the shifting votes of doubtful members and the identity of the eight missing members should be considered in interpreting this division. The approximately equal division between those favoring and those opposing repeal in each party meant that the final decision rested with the votes of a few doubtful members. These votes were affected by a compromise in the bill itself and by external pressure.

In addition, the debate in Congress played an important role in influencing Congressmen's attitudes. One personal influence should be mentioned as he played a fundamental strategic role in the repeal campaign. Walter Judd, Republican from Minnesota, testified before the House Committee on May 20, 1943, and his testimony ran to over twenty-seven pages in the House *Hearings*. In the House debate, his remarks occupy more than eighty pages in the *Congressional Record*.[42] No other member of the House spoke so much for the repeal. Yet his contribution cannot be judged in terms of speeches. In practice it operated on a much deeper level.

Judd's background gave him deep conviction on this subject. After twelve years of service in China as a medical missionary, he had resigned to campaign in America against aiding Japan in her war on China, and finally decided to run for Congress in 1942.[43] Before taking his seat for the first time in Washington, he had already determined to fight for the repeal of the Asian exclusion law stressed this was one of the main reasons for his decision to run for Congress.[44] He communicated with private leaders and worked out plans for action as the situation evolved.

As events developed during the session, Judd worked closely with other interested Congressmen in devising a strategy by which the repeal movement could succeed. At first he thought of introducing a bill himself, but as he studied the situation more intimately, he realized that this was not the best way to ensure passage. The sponsor, he felt, should belong to the Democratic majority party, and should come either from the South or West where opposition was likely to be greatest. Gossett and Magnuson not only fulfilled these qualifications, but were men with prestige, skill and experience. Of greatest significance than his speeches before the Committee and the House were the long hours Judd spent in personal discussion with key members of Congress attempting to win their support for the bill. He was the most energetic young Congressman to work for the passage of the Magnuson Act.[45]

Finally, the support of President Roosevelt was a decisive element in the success of the repeal movement. On October 10, 1943, when the House began a general debate on the Chinese issue, a number of Congressmen expressed strong opposition for the repeal. For example, William P. Elmer (Republican, Missouri) urged Congress to "tighten instead of losing our immigration laws" in order to "keep America for Americans."[46]

In the midst of this heated debate, President Roosevelt sent a special message to Congress in support of repeal. He pointed out that the repeal of the Chinese Exclusion Acts would silence "distorted Japanese propaganda." Roosevelt argued that the symbolic number of Chinese who could enter the country would neither cause unemployment nor provide competition. In addition, he regarded the new immigration legislation "as important in the cause of winning the war and of establishing a secure peace." Since China was America's ally and her resistance depended, in part, on "the spirit of her people and her faith in her allies." President Roosevelt argued for a show of support and stated:

> There is now pending before the Congress legislation to the immigration of Chinese people into this country and to allow Chinese residents here to become American citizens. I regard this legislation an important in the cause of winning the war and of establishing a secure peace.... China is our ally. For many long years she stood alone in the fight against aggression. Today

we fight at her side. She has continued her gallant struggle against very great odds......

Nations, like individuals, make mistake. We must be big enough to acknowledge our mistakes of the past and to correct them. By the repeal of the Chinese exclusion laws, we can correct a historic mistake and silence the distorted Japanese propaganda....

The extension of the privileges of citizenship to the relatively few Chinese residents in our country would operate as another meaningful display of friendship. It would be additional proof that we regard China not only as a partner in waging war but that we shall regard her as a partner in days of peace. While it would give the Chinese a preferred status over certain other oriental people, their great contribution to the cause of decency and freedom entitles them to such preference.[47]

In his speech, Roosevelt laid primary stress on the foreign-policy aspects of repeal. He urged Congress should "correct an injustice to our friends" and "now will be an earnest of our purpose to apply the policy of the good neighbor to our relations with other peoples."

Nine bills modifying the Chinese Exclusion Acts were introduced into Congress in 1943. The broadest bill, introduced by New York City Representative Vito Marcantonio, would have made the naturalization status totally color blind and was never seriously considered. The House finally focused on a measure introduced by Warren Magnuson (Democrat, Washington) which was debated and passed by the House in October. The act was a simple one, in three sections. Section one repealed all Chinese exclusion acts enacted between 1882 and 1913. Section two gave a quota to "persons of the Chinese race" which, under the law, was set at 105 annually. Section three amended the nationality act to make "Chinese persons or persons of Chinese descent" eligible for naturalization on the same terms as other immigrants.[48] On November 26, the Senate approved the repeal of the Chinese Exclusion Acts. On December 17, President Roosevelt signed the bill which had constituted an integral part of American immigration policy for over sixty years.

Note

[1] Confidential U.S. State Department Central Files, United States –China Relations, 1940-1949, Vol. 1, National Archives, Washington D.C. (Hereafter cited as Central Files)

[2] *Ibid.*

[3] *Ibid.*

[4] *Ibid.*

[5] *Ibid.*

[6] *Ibid.*

[7] Memorandum by the Chief of the Division of Far Eastern Affairs (Maxwell M. Hamilton), "China's War Potential: Estimate," June 17, 1942, *FRUS*, 1942 (China), pp.71-79.

[8] *Ibid.*

[9] Memorandum by the Chief of the Division of Far Eastern Affairs (Maxwell M. Hamilton), February 27, 1943, *FRUS*, 1943 (China), p.14.

[10] *Ibid.*

[11] Memorandum of Conversation by Breckingridge Long (Assistant Secretary of State), October 2, 1943, Central Files.

[12] Memorandum of Conversation by the Assistant Secretary of State (Breckingridge Long), May 13, 1943, *FRUS*, 1943 (China), pp.770-771.

[13] U.S. Congress, *Congressional Record*, 78th Congress, 1st Session, Vol.89, Part 9, p.634.

[14] *Ibid*, p.1136.

[15] Memorandum, May 18, 1943, Papers of Minutes Committee on Immigration and Naturalization, House of Representatives, U.S. Congress. National Archives, Washington, D.C.

[16] House *Hearings*, 1943, pp.178-180.

[17] *Ibid*, p.177.

[18] *Ibid*, pp.184-186.

[19] *Ibid*, p.183.

[20] *Ibid*, pp.184-185.

[21] *Ibid*, p.183.

[22] *Ibid*, pp.68-86.

[23] *Ibid*, p.70.

[24] Charles G. Finney, *The Old China Hands* (Westport, Connecticut: Greenwood Press, 1973).

[25] Fred W. Riggs, *Pressures on Congress: A Study of the Repeal of Chinese Exclusion*, p.108.

[26] House *Hearings*, 1943, pp.227-233.

[27] *Ibid*, p.234.

[28] *Ibid*, pp.150-151.

[29] *Ibid*, pp.248-249.

[30] U.S. Congress, *Congressional Record*, 78th Congress, 1st Session, Vol.89, Part 9, p.4427.

[31] The Under Secretary (Edward R. Stettinius) to the Speaker of the House of Representatives (Sam Rayburn), October 27, 1943, *FRUS*, 1943 (China), pp.783-784.

[32] Robert Dallek, *Franklin D. Roosevelt and American Foreign Policy, 1932-1945* (New York, 1979), p.390.

[33] Joseph W. Stilwell, *The Stilwell Papers* (New York, 1948), p.240.

[34] "Report from the Nation, December 7, 1941-December 7, 1942," President Secretary's File, Box 156, Franklin D. Roosevelt Papers, Franklin D. Roosevelt Library, Hyde Park, New York.

[35] Memorandum of Conversation between Chiang Kai-shek and Wendell L. Willkie, October 5, 1942, Qing Xiao-yi, ed., *Zhonghuaminguo zhongyao shiliao chubian: Duiri kanzhan shiqi* [Important Historical Documents of the Republic of China: During the Period of the Anti-Japanese War] Part 3, Vol.1 (Taibei, 1981), p.762. (Hereafter cited as *ZZSC*.)

[36] *Ibid.*

[37] Robert E. Sherwood, *Roosevelt and Hopkins: An Intimate History* (New York, 1948), p.706.

[38] Qing Xiao-yi, ed., *ZZSC*, Part 3, Vol.3, p.832.

[39] Fred W. Riggs, *Pressures on Congress: A Study of the Repeal of Chinese Exclusion*, pp.167-168.

[40] Henry L. Feingold, *The Jewish People in America: A Time for Searching - Entering the Mainstream, 1920-1945* (Baltimore, Maryland: John Hopkins University Press, 1992), pp.28-28, and p.194.

[41] Report of October, House of Representatives, Papers of Minutes Committee on Immigration and Naturalization, 1943, National Archives, Washington D.C..

[42] House *Hearings*, 1943, pp.142-167; U.S. Congress, *Congressional*

Record, 78th Congress, 1st Session, Vol.89, Part 6, pp.8588-8593..

[43] Edwards Lee, *Missionary for Freedom: The Life and Times of Walter Judd* (New York: Paragon House, 1990); Yanli Gao, "Judd's China: A Missionary Congressman and US-China Policy," *Journal of Modern Chinese History*, December 2008, Vol.2, pp.197-219.

[44] Walter Judd, "Should We Repeal the Chinese Exclusion Laws Now?" addressed at Town Meeting of the Air, September 2, 1943, Papers of Walter Judd, Hoover Institution, Stanford University.

[45] For Walter Judd's role in the repeal campaign, see Xiaohua Ma, *Maboroshino shinchitsujo to ajia taiheiyo: Dainiji seikai taisenki no beichu domei no atsureki* [Illusionary Orders in the Asia-Pacific: The Chinese American Alliance in the War Against Japan (Tokyo: Sairyuusha, 2000), Chapter 5.

[46] U.S. Congress, *Congressional Record*, 78th Congress, 1st Session, Vol.89, Part 6, p.8595.

[47] Speech of Franklin D. Roosevelt Message to Congress, October 11, 1943, National Archives, Washington, D.C.

[48] Fred W. Riggs, *Pressures on Congress: A Study of the Repeal of Chinese Exclusion*, p.137.

Conclusion

The outbreak of the Pacific War threw the spot light on the Chinese Exclusion Acts and cleared the path for a new direction in American immigration history. To some extent, the repeal of the Chinese Exclusion Acts gave the Chinese technical equality, in granting them a symbolic quota per annum and allowing Chinese immigrants to acquire American citizenship. From this point of view, the repeal of the anti-Chinese immigration laws marked a turning point in American history, since they codified, for the first time, the idea that Chinese immigrants were "assimilable" into American society, despite the fact that the quota granted to them was at first only symbolic.

Even more important than the changes in law were the changes of American ideology. The United States was still patently a white man's country in wartime. However, the notion was beginning to prevail that equal opportunity ought to be given at least lip service. Japanese wartime racial propaganda, which denounced American racism and the humiliating treatment of the Chinese immigrants, forced Americans to look critically at the racism within their society. In fighting a propaganda war, Americans realized that they must stand before the whole world in support of racial tolerance and equality.

On the other hand, before the war, as we have seen, the Chinese American community was largely shut out of the mainstream of American society due to discriminatory laws. Changes in wartime attitudes towards the Chinese accompanied a steady improvement of the image and reputation of Chinese-Americans, particularly their efforts in the war against Japanese aggression. During World War II, the changes of the American image of the Chinese had been almost all positive. Thus, the war created a favorable climate for Chinese Americans to be accepted by American society.

Although the majority of Chinese-Americans had grown up in the United States, racial prejudice and discriminatory legislation against the Chinese before the war had prevented their participation in many areas of American society. It was the war that opened the door for Chinese-Americans to participate in many fields of American society. A great number of Chinese-Americans were needed for the nation's armed forces and defense industries. According to U.S. Military Service data, almost 16,000 Chinese-Americans served in the U.S. military between 1940 and 1946. About 1,600 even serviced in the U.S. Navy, some in commission ranks.[1] Thus, for the first time, Chinese-Americans began to be accepted by the larger American society. The Chinese-American "success" in the war fighting for democracy and freedom won high praise from the American society and enabled them to be "the Model Minority" in post war era. Therefore, the war all combined to transform American attitudes from what American historian Harold R. Isaacs had called the "Age of Contempt" into the "Age of Admiration."[2]

Nevertheless, the repeal itself did not place Chinese on full quota parity with other European countries eligible for immigration and citizenship. In fact, traditional nativism endured and played a significant role in the repeal debate. According to a Gallup Poll carried out in November 1943, the month after the House passed the repealing bill, the approval/disapproval rate was quite close, forty-two to forty.[3] Racism against the Asians was as consistently expressed in the repeal movement in 1943 as it was in the passage of the Chinese Exclusion Act in 1882. Undoubtedly, the continuance of strong racism during wartime impeded the development of the repeal campaign.

The strategic significance of the repeal, however, went far beyond the repeal itself. In 1943, China's precarious military and political situation was extremely reinforced, while the political and military necessities made psychological gestures appear more significant than ever before. Meantime, the wartime enthusiasm for China, dramatized by Mme. Chiang Kai-shek's national tour, made it difficult to resist efforts to support China. Furthermore, China's postwar cooperation with the United States in America's global strategy became increasingly indispensable. Overall, the repeal represented an important public gesture from the United States to its ally China, and also from one Allied nation to an Axis enemy.

Therefore the repeal of Chinese Exclusion was significant because it would at least symbolically redefine in the words of the face of a nation. It became an essential prerequisite for America's policy to promote China as a "Great Power" because the United States sought to keep an "equal" partner in postwar Asia so that the American vision of a "strong," "democratic" and American-oriented

123

China could emerge in the postwar world. This implies that the repeal of the Chinese Exclusion Acts was not only the result of America's wartime strategy, but also a reflection of its long-term goals for East Asian policy in the postwar era.

Most importantly, the repeal of the Chinese Exclusion Acts paved the way for measures in 1946 to admit other Asian people, for example Filipino and Indian immigrants to enter the country. The exclusion of these groups had long damaged U.S. relations with the Philippines and India. It was on the basis of these same political and military strategies that other anti-Asian laws, such as those targeting Indians and Filipinos, were removed, although the act followed the pattern of the Chinese quota and assigned racial, not national, quotas to all Asian immigrants. Eventually, the U.S. Congress enacted the McCarran-Walter Immigration Act in 1952.

However, as was the case in the repeal of Chinese exclusion, these acts did not alter the racially discriminatory treatment of Asian people. While repeal purportedly removed racial discrimination from American immigration laws, it did not directly confront American racism because it was not passed primarily for the benefit of Chinese or Asian Americans residing in the United States. The question of American citizenship for Chinese immigrants involved discussion of whether Americans wanted Chinese not only as their friends across the Pacific, but as neighbors across the fence in their communities. As the repeal campaign demonstrated that most Americans widely acknowledged the desirability of repealing the Chinese Exclusion Acts as a foreign policy measure. Yet, they are much more hesitant to welcome Chinese into the American national community. In fact a repeal bill introduced by Congressman Ed Gossett (Democrat, Texas) had been considered at the end of the first session in June 1943, because a majority of the House Committee agreed on the necessity to terminate the exclusion acts. Controversy, however, occurred when the issue on allowing Chinese to enter the United States under the quota system was discussed. Understanding the sentiment, the Citizens Committee changed its strategy and emphasized that the repeal would allow only a minimum number of Chinese immigrants to enter the country while providing important gesture of respect for China, American ally in Asia.

Even President Roosevelt himself emphasized that the "Chinese quota would be only about 100 immigrants a year" and "such number of immigrants will not cause unemployment or provide competition in the search of a job."[4] When President Roosevelt signed the bill into the law on December 17, 1943, he reiterated its foreign-policy implication as a war measure affecting mostly persons abroad rather than as a redress of Chinese-American grievance. Underscoring the lack of concern for the problems of Chinese-Americans, as opposed to those of China, is the fact that the Citizens Committee, the Congress, and the president steadily ignored the bills introduced by Congressman John Lesinski (Democrat, Michigan) on February 1, 1943 and others which would have allowed the alien wives of Chinese-American citizens to enter the United States as citizens.[5] Family unification later became a prime factor in immigration reform but was not considered crucial in 1943, at least not for Asian families.

At the same time, some forms of legal discrimination against the Chinese immigrants still exited in American society despite the fact that the exclusion acts were repealed. For example, California state laws prohibited Chinese immigrants from marrying whites and other states had anti-miscegenation laws until 1967, although the United States Supreme Court unanimously proclaimed that those laws are unconstitutional.[6] It would take another decade before Asian immigrants could achieve full equality in American legislation.

After World War II, especially as a result of the Civil Rights Movement in the 1960s, a legislative reform to repeal the Immigration Law of 1924, which was based on Anglo-Saxonism to exclude Asians to enter to the United States, started. In 1965, a new law of immigration and naturalization, known as Hart-Celler Act, was enacted by U.S. Congress. The Immigration and Naturalization Act of 1965 abolished the National Origins Formula that had structured American immigration police since 1920s and removed discriminatory restrictions on Asian immigration to the United States. This act was proposed by Senator Philip Hart (Democrat, Michigan) and Ted Kennedy (Democrat, Massachusetts), supported by a Hawaii-born Chinese-American Senator, Hiram Fong, the first Asian American Senator in U.S. history. The new immigration law of 1965 not only placed Asian peoples on a full quota parity with European peoples eligible for immigration and citizenship, but also became a milestone in American immigration history. It marked the beginning

126

of a new era of racial tolerance and coming of a new century of coexistence of multiculturalism.

Figure 29: A Chinese-American Fighting for Equality

Hiram Fong, a Hawaii-born Chinese-American, served as a major in the United States Army Air Force during World War II and later became the first Chinese-American Senator (1959-1977) in the U.S. Congress.

(Source: University of Hawaii at Manoa Library)

Figure 30: Hiram Fong's Proposal for the Immigration Reform in the Senate Subcommittee on Immigration and Naturalization

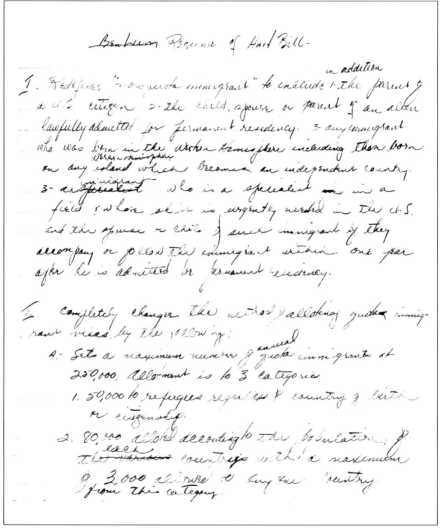

(Source: University of Hawaii at Manoa Library)

3. 120,000 alloted by comparing the total number of quota and non-quota immigrants from each country with the total number of quota & non-quota immigrants allowed into the U.S. during the past 15 years.

The maximum any country can receive during any one year is 25,000 - minimum is 200.

Applicants are awarded a quota in 2 ways.
1. Country of birth
2. Country of citizenship - however, to qualify the applicant must have resided 10 or more years in such country.

Any quota not used by a country during any one year is put into a pool. Countries having a backlog of applicants may draw from this pool, but may not draw more than its total annual quota. The maximum a country may draw from the pool is

Figure 31: Senator Hiram Fong and Japanese Americans

(Source: University of Hawaii at Manoa Library)

Hiram Fong was one of Hawaii's first two U.S. Senators when the Territory became a State in 1959. He came from a poor immigrant family but became the first resident to receive the Horatio Alger Award for overcoming poverty to achieve outstanding success in business and public service. Fong graduated from Harvard Law School in 1935 and became the first U.S. Senator of Asian ancestry. During his 18 years in the Senate, Senator Fong advocated civil rights and voting rights legislation. In 1963, Fong was one of seven Republicans to introduce a package of civil rights legislation in the U.S. Senate and supported President Lyndon Johnson's Voting Rights Act of 1965.

Being the first Asian American Minority Member to serve on the Senate Judiciary Committee and Senate Subcommittee on Immigration and Naturalization, Senator Fong was in the forefront in the fight to eliminate discrimination against Asians. He was particularly instrumental in the elimination based on national origin quotas in the bill which became the Immigration Act of 1965, also known as the Hart-Celler Act of 1965. He testified before the hearings of Senate Subcommittee on Immigration and Naturalization on February 24, 1965, requesting the Congress to seek "an immigration policy reflecting America's ideal of the equality of all men without regard to race, color, creed, or national origin" so that "we could enhance America's image as leader of the free world in according equal dignity and respect to all peoples of the world, and thus accomplish a significant forward stride in our international relations."[7]

In 1964, Senator Fong became the first Asian American to run for his party's nomination for President of the United States and ran for U.S. President in 1968 again. He was the only Asian American to actively seek the Presidential nomination of the Republican Party. Senator Fong also played a significant role in the passage of Japan-US Friendship Act of 1975.

Figure 32: Senator Fong in the Presidential Election Campaign

(Source: University of Hawaii at Manoa Library)

Figure 33: Hiram Fong for President Pinback

(Source: University of Hawaii at Manoa Library)

The impact of the 1965 act on Asian Americans cannot be denied. The most important aspect of the Immigration and Naturalization Act of 1965 was that it essentially reorganized the immigration system to favor family reunification and opened the door to immigration from Asian countries. During the period between 1921 and 1960, Asian immigration constituted less than 4 percent of total U.S. immigration.

After the Immigration and Naturalization Act of 1965, Asian

immigrants represented 35 percent of the total U.S. immigration from 1971 to 1980 and 42 percent from 1981 to 1989. The sudden large flux of immigration as a result of the Immigration Act of 1965 had a profound impact on Asian American community and politics. Although Chinese-Americans constitutes a small percentage of the U.S. population, their numbers are steadily increasing - from less than 240,000 in 1960 to approximately four million today, about 1.2 percent of the total U.S. population.

The Chinese-American experience during World War II is merely one example of how American view of Asians had changed. Chinese-Americans have experienced much racial subjugation and discrimination in American history. Despite numerous barriers, Chinese-Americans have begun to be involved in American politics and have continuously fought against discrimination.

Due to their efforts, U.S. Congress passed a resolution on June 18, 2012, which formally expressed the regret of the enactment of the Chinese Exclusion Acts. The resolution had been approved by the U.S. Senate in October 2012. Despite such an improvement, Chinese-Americans still have a long way to go before full equality is achieved in the United States.

Note

[1] Roger Daniels, *Asian America: Chinese and Japanese in the United States since 1850* (Seattle: University of Washington Press, 1988), pp.299-300.

[2] Harold R. Isaacs, *Scratches on Our Minds: American Images of China and India* (New York: Praeger, 1973), p.71.

[3] *The New York Times*, November 21, 1943.

[4] Speech of President Franklin D. Roosevelt to Congress on October 11, 1943, National Archives, Washington, D.C.

[5] U.S. Congress, House of Representatives, *A Bill to Provide for the Admission to the United States of Alien Chinese Wives of American Citizens.* H.R. 1607, 78th Congress, 1st Session, 1943, p.1.

[6] Gabriel Chin and Hrish Karthikeyan, "Preserving Racial Identity: Population Patterns and the Application on Anti-Miscegeneration Statutes to Asian Americans, 1910-1950, *Asian Law Journal* (Social Science Research Network), May 5, 2014.

[7] "Testimony on S. 500 -- Immigration Revisions" by Senator Hiram L. Fong, R Hawaii, before Senate Subcommittee on Immigration, February 24, 1965, Senator Hiram Fong Papers, University of Hawaii at Manoa Library, Hawaii.

Appendixes

i . The Magnuson Act of 1943

Seventy-eighth Congress of the United States of America;

At the First Session

Begun and held at the City of Washington on Wednesday, the sixth
day of January, one thousand nine hundred and forty-three

AN ACT

To repeal the Chinese Exclusion Acts, to establish quotas, and for
other purposes.

*Be it enacted by the Senate and House of Representatives of the
United States of America in Congress assembled,* That the following
Acts or parts of Acts relating to the exclusion or deportation of
persons of the Chinese race are hereby repealed: May 6, 1882 (22 Stat.
L. 58) ; July 5, 1884 (23 Stat. L. 115) ; September 13, 1888 (25 Stat.
L. 476) ; October 1, 1888 (25 Stat. L. 504) ; May 5, 1892 (27 Stat. L.
25) ; November 3, 1893 (28 Stat. L. 7) ; that portion of section 1 of
the Act of July 7, 1898 (30 Stat. L. 750, 751), which reads as follows:
"There shall be no further immigration of Chinese into the Hawaiian
Islands except upon such conditions as are now or may hereafter be
allowed by the laws of the United States; and no Chinese, by reason
of anything herein contained, shall be allowed to enter the United
States from the Hawaiian Islands."; section 101 of the Act of April
30, 1900 (31 Stat. L. 141, 161) ; those portions of section 1 of the Act
of June 6, 1900 (31 Stat. L. 588, 611), which read as follows: "And
nothing in section four of the Act of August fifth, eighteen hundred
and eighty-two (Twenty-second Statutes at Large, page two hundred
and twenty-five), shall be construed to prevent the Secretary of the
Treasury from hereafter detailing one officer employed in the enforcement of the Chinese Exclusion Acts for duty at the Treasury Department at Washington. * * * and hereafter the Commissioner-
General of Immigration, in addition to his other duties, shall have
charge of the administration of the Chinese exclusion law * * *,
under the supervision and direction of the Secretary of the Treasury."; March 3, 1901 (31 Stat. L. 1093) ; April 29, 1902 (32 Stat. L.
176) ; April 27, 1904 (33 Stat. L. 428) ; section 25 of the Act of
March 3, 1911 (36 Stat. L. 1087, 1094) ; that portion of the Act of
August 24, 1912 (37 Stat. L. 417, 476), which reads as follows:
"*Provided,* That all charges for maintenance or return of Chinese
persons applying for admission to the United States shall hereafter
be paid or reimbursed to the United States by the person, company,
partnership, or corporation, bringing such Chinese to a port of the
United States as applicants for admission."; that portion of the Act
of June 23, 1913 (38 Stat. L. 4, 65), which reads as follows: "*Pro-*

(U.S. National Archives)

H. R. 3070——2

vided, That from and after July first, nineteen hundred and thirteen, all Chinese persons ordered deported under judicial writs shall be delivered by the marshal of the district or his deputy into the custody of any officer designated for that purpose by the Secretary of Commerce and Labor, for conveyance to the frontier or seaboard for deportation in the same manner as aliens deported under the immigration laws."

Sec. 2. With the exception of those coming under subsections (b), (d), (e), and (f) of section 4, Immigration Act of 1924 (43 Stat. 155; 44 Stat. 812; 45 Stat. 1009; 46 Stat. 854; 47 Stat. 656; 8 U. S. C. 204), all Chinese persons entering the United States annually as immigrants shall be allocated to the quota for the Chinese computed under the provisions of section 11 of the said Act. A preference up to 75 per centum of the quota shall be given to Chinese born and resident in China.

Sec. 3. Section 303 of the Nationality Act of 1940, as amended (54 Stat. 1140; 8 U. S. C. 703), is hereby amended by striking out the word "and" before the word "descendants", changing the colon after the word "Hemisphere" to a comma, and adding the following: "and Chinese persons or persons of Chinese descent :".

Speaker of the House of Representatives.

Vice President of the United States and
President of the Senate.

Approved
Dec 17 1943
Franklin D Roosevelt

137

ⅱ. Summary of Chinese Exclusion Acts

This section sets forth the features of the laws relating to the exclusion of the Chinese in the United States. It does not purport to be exhaustive, but is devised to present, as briefly and as clearly as possible, a comprehensive statement of the important provisions in the U.S. legislation.

1. Act of May 6, 1882 (the basic Chinese Exclusion Act)
   (1) Suspended immigrants of Chinese laborers for ten years.
   (2) Permitted Chinese laborers resident in the United States, to obtain certificate from the collector of customs entitling them to return to the United States after temporary absence.
   (3) Chinese persons other than laborers could be admitted to the United States upon production of a certificate from the Chinese government in the English language, describing the immigrant and certifying to his right to come to the United States under the terms of the treaty with China. This document known as the Section Six Certificate, was to be the prima facie evidence of the facts therein stated.
   (4) Chinese persons who entered the United States improperly after the passage of the act were to be deported upon order of a judge or commissioner of a court of the United States.
   (5) "That hereafter no State court or court of the United States shall admit Chinese Citizenship."

2. **Act of July 5, 1884 (amended the Act of May 6, 1882)**
   (1) Section Six Certificate could be issued by any foreign government of which Chinese person was then subject.
   (2) Section Six Certificate required an antecedent visa at the place of departure by the American consul, who was instructed to inquire into the veracity of the statements in the certificate and to refuse his visa where he found the statements untrue. It was also provided that the Section Six Certificate should be "the sole evidence permissible on the part of the person so producing the same to establish a right of entry into the United States; but said certificate may be controverted and the facts therein stated disproved by the United States authorities."

3. **Act of September 13, 1888**

   A Chinese laborer who departed from the United States was not permitted to return unless he had a lawful wife, child, or parent in the United States, or property therein valued at $1,000. A Chinese laborer within these exemptions who desired to depart temporarily was required to obtain from the local collector of customs a return certificate which was valid for one year and could be extended for a further one-year period only in certain contingencies.

4. **Act of October 1, 1888 (known as the Scott Act)**
   (1) Prohibited return of any Chinese laborers who departed from the United States.
   (2) Forbade the issuance of return certificates to Chinese laborers resident in the United States and canceled outstanding return

certificates which had been issued under sections 4 and 5 of the Act of May 5, 1882, to Chinese laborers in the United States who had left this country on temporary visits abroad.

5. **Act of May 5, 1892 (known as the Geary Act)**
   (1) Extended all Chinese exclusion acts for a period of ten years.
   (2) Placed on Chinese persons apprehended in deportation proceedings the burden of establishing their lawful right to remain in the United States.
   (3) Prohibited allowance of bail to Chinese persons who had been denied privilege of landing in the United States and who thereafter brought habeas corpus proceedings.
   (4) Required registration within one year of all Chinese laborers then in the United States and provided for the issuance of certificates of residence to those who could establish the legality of their presence in the United States, and were to be deported upon order of a United States judge, unless they satisfied such judge 1) that the failure to obtain the certificate of residence was caused by accident, sickness, or other unavoidable cause, and 2) that they were resident in the United States on May 5, 1892, which fact had to be proved by the testimony of at least one credible white witness.

6. **Act of November 3, 1893 (amended the Act of May 5, 1892)**
   (1) Extended time for registration of Chinese laborers for six months.
   (2) Defined "laborer" and "merchant" as those terms are used in the Chinese exclusion laws.

(3) Prohibited release on bail of Chinese persons under order of deportation.

7. Act of July 7, 1898

Prohibited further immigration of Chinese into Hawaiian Islands except upon such conditions as they were admissible to the United States.

8. Act of April 30, 1900

Required Chinese then in Hawaii to register and obtain certificates of residence within one year in same manner as required under Act of May 5, 1892.

9. Act of June 6, 1900

Authorized detailing of one officer to specialize in enforcement of Chinese exclusion acts in Treasury (now Justice) Department, and directing that Commissioner General of Immigration (now Commissioner of Immigration and Naturalization) shall have charge of enforcement of Chinese exclusion laws.

10. Act of March 3, 1901

No warrant of arrest for violation of Chinese exclusion laws to be issued except upon sworn complaint of designated government officials, unless the issuing of such warrant of arrest shall first be approved or requested in writing by the United States attorney of the district in which the warrant is issued.

11. Act of April 29, 1902

(1) Extended all Chinese exclusion laws then in force, so far as same were not inconsistent with treaty obligation.

(2) Required registration and obtaining of certificates of residence by Chinese persons in insular possession of the United States.

12. Act of April 27, 1904

Extended all Chinese exclusion laws without any further limitation in time, made such laws applicable to the island territory under the jurisdiction of the United States, and prohibited immigration of Chinese laborers from such island territory of the United States to the mainland territory of the United States.

13. Act of March 3, 1911

Conferred appellate jurisdiction on the United States district courts of the judgments and orders of the United States commissioners in cases arising under the Chinese exclusion laws.

14. Act of August 24, 1912

Reimbursement for all charges for maintenance or return of Chinese persons applying for admission to the United States to be made to the United States by the person, company, partnership, or corporation bringing such persons to a port of the United States as applicants for admission.

15. Act of June 23, 1913

All Chinese persons ordered deported under judicial writs to be delivered by the United States marshal to custody of officers of the

Immigration and Naturalization Service, for deportation in the same manner as aliens deported under the immigration laws.

ⅲ. Chronology of Legislative Process of the Repeal of the Chinese Exclusion Acts (1943-1944)

Year of 1943

Feb. 1   H. R. 1607.

Introduced by John Lesinski (Democrat, Michigan).

"To provide for the admission to the United States of alien Chinese wives of American citizens...."

Feb.17   H. R. 1881.

Introduced by Martin Kennedy (Democrat, New York).

"Chinese citizenship act of 1943"

(Would repeal Chinese Exclusion Acts and make Chinese eligible for naturalization)

Feb.26   H. R. 2011.

Introduced by Vito Anthony Marcantonio (Republican, New York).

"To amend the Nationality Act of 1940."

(Would have provided that "the right of a person to become a naturalized citizen of the United States shall not be denied or abridged because of race, color, creed, or national origin."

Mar. 26   H. R. 2309.

Introduced by Warren Magnuson (Democrat, Washington).

"To amend the Immigration Act of 1924, as amended, to provide that aliens who are subjects of China shall be admitted into the United States under such act."

(Would simply have added a new section to the law providing for the admission of Chinese immigrants under a quota determined by citizenship and residence in China.)

April 7 H. R. 2428.

Introduced by Samuel Dickstein (Democrat, New York, Chairman of House Committee on Immigration and Naturalization).

"To repeal the Chinese Exclusion Laws and to abrogate the Treaty of 1880."

April 7 H. R. 2429.

Introduced by Samuel Dickstein.

"To repeal the Chinese Exclusion Laws."

May 19-20 House Hearings

House Committee on Immigration and Naturalization, on H. R. 1882 and 2309.

May 26-27 House Hearings, continued.

June 2-3 House Hearings, concluded.

June 7 Executive session of House Committee, majority in straw vote favors simple repeal, no majority for quota.

June 7 H. R. 2892.

Introduced by Ed Gossett (Democrat, Texas).

"To repeal the Chinese Exclusion laws, to place Chinese on a quota basis, and to repeal the laws denying the Chinese the right to become citizens of the United States."

June 14 H. R. 2942.

Introduced by Ed Gossett.

"To reduce immigration, and to repeal the Chinese Exclusion Laws...."

June 29 H. R. 3070.

Introduced by Warren Magnuson.

"An act to repeal the Chinese Exclusion Acts, to establish quotas, and for other purposes."

Summer Recess

Sept.30   S. 1404. (Identical with H. R. 3070)
Introduced by Charles C. Andrews (Democrat, Florida).

Oct. 7   House Report 732.
Introduced by Samuel Dickstein.
Favorable report on H. R. 3070.

Oct.11   House Report 735. (Minority Report)
Introduced by Marion Tinsley Bennett (Republican, Missouri).
Report from Rules Committee on House H. R. 3070, with House Resolution 314.

Oct.11   President Franklin D. Roosevelt sent a message to Congress

Oct.20   House.
General debate.

Oct.21   House.
Debate and passed.

Nov. 4   Senate. Subcommittee of Immigration Committee passed.

Nov.16   Senate Report 535.
Introduced by Charles C. Andrews.
Favorable report on H. R. 3070.

Nov.26   Senate.
Debate and passed.

Dec.17   President Franklin D. Roosevelt signed.

Year of 1944

Feb.9   Proclamation 2603.

Fixing Chinese quota at 105.

iv. **House Resolution of June 18, 2012**

112TH CONGRESS
2D SESSION
H. RES. 683

Expressing the regret of the House of Representatives for the passage of laws that adversely affected the Chinese in the United States, including the Chinese Exclusion Act.

IN THE HOUSE OF REPRESENTATIVES

JUNE 8, 2012

Ms. CHU (for herself, Mr. SMITH of Texas, Mr. HONDA, Mr. ISSA, Mr. BURTON of Indiana, Mr. CLAY, Ms. LEE of California, Mr. GRIJALVA, Mr. SCHIFF, and Mr. JACKSON of Illinois) submitted the following resolution; which was referred to the Committee on the Judiciary

---

RESOLUTION

Expressing the regret of the House of Representatives for the passage of laws that adversely affected the Chinese in the United States, including the Chinese Exclusion Act.

Whereas many Chinese came to the United States in the 19th and 20th centuries, as did people from other countries, in search of the opportunity to create a better life;

Whereas the United States ratified the Burlingame Treaty on October 19, 1868, which permitted the free movement of the Chinese people to, from, and within the United States and made China a "most favored nation";

Whereas in 1878, the House of Representatives passed a resolution requesting that President Rutherford B. Hayes

2

renegotiate the Burlingame Treaty so Congress could limit Chinese immigration to the United States;

Whereas, on February 22, 1879, the House of Representatives passed the Fifteen Passenger Bill, which only permitted 15 Chinese passengers on any ship coming to the United States;

Whereas, on March 1, 1879, President Hayes vetoed the Fifteen Passenger Bill as being incompatible with the Burlingame Treaty;

Whereas, on May 9, 1881, the United States ratified the Angell Treaty, which allowed the United States to suspend, but not prohibit, immigration of Chinese laborers, declared that "Chinese laborers who are now in the United States shall be allowed to go and come of their own free will," and reaffirmed that Chinese persons possessed "all the rights, privileges, immunities, and exemptions which are accorded to the citizens and subjects of the most favored nation";

Whereas the House of Representatives passed legislation that adversely affected Chinese persons in the United States and limited their civil rights, including—

(1) on March 23, 1882, the first Chinese Exclusion bill, which excluded for 20 years skilled and unskilled Chinese laborers and expressly denied Chinese persons alone the right to be naturalized as American citizens, and which was opposed by President Chester A. Arthur as incompatible with the terms and spirit of the Angell Treaty;

(2) on April 17, 1882, intending to address President Arthur's concerns, the House passed a new Chinese Exclusion bill, which prohibited Chinese workers from entering the United States for 10 years instead of 20, re-

•HRES 683 IH

149

quired certain Chinese laborers already legally present in the United States who later wished to reenter the United States to obtain "certificates of return," and prohibited courts from naturalizing Chinese individuals;

(3) on May 3, 1884, an expansion of the Chinese Exclusion Act, which applied it to all persons of Chinese descent, "whether subjects of China or any other foreign power";

(4) on September 3, 1888, the Scott Act, which prohibited legal Chinese laborers from reentering the United States and cancelled all previously issued "certificates of return," and which was later determined by the Supreme Court to have abrogated the Angell Treaty; and

(5) on April 4, 1892, the Geary Act, which reauthorized the Chinese Exclusion Act for another ten years, denied Chinese immigrants the right to be released on bail upon application for a writ of habeas corpus, and contrary to customary legal standards regarding the presumption of innocence, authorized the deportation of Chinese persons who could not produce a certificate of residence unless they could establish residence through the testimony of "at least one credible white witness";

Whereas in the 1894 Gresham-Yang Treaty, the Chinese government consented to a prohibition of Chinese immigration and the enforcement of the Geary Act in exchange for readmission to the United States of Chinese persons who were United States residents;

Whereas in 1898, the United States annexed Hawaii, took control of the Philippines, and excluded only the residents of Chinese ancestry of these territories from entering the United States mainland;

•HRES 683 IH

4

Whereas, on April 29, 1902, as the Geary Act was expiring, Congress indefinitely extended all laws regulating and restricting Chinese immigration and residence, to the extent consistent with Treaty commitments;

Whereas in 1904, after the Chinese government withdrew from the Gresham-Yang Treaty, Congress permanently extended, "without modification, limitation, or condition," the prohibition on Chinese naturalization and immigration;

Whereas these Federal statutes enshrined in law the exclusion of the Chinese from the democratic process and the promise of American freedom;

Whereas in an attempt to undermine the American-Chinese alliance during World War II, enemy forces used the Chinese exclusion legislation passed in Congress as evidence of anti-Chinese attitudes in the United States;

Whereas in 1943, in furtherance of American war objectives, at the urging of President Franklin D. Roosevelt, Congress repealed previously enacted legislation and permitted Chinese persons to become United States citizens;

Whereas Chinese-Americans continue to play a significant role in the success of the United States; and

Whereas the United States was founded on the principle that all persons are created equal: Now, therefore, be it

1   *Resolved,*

2   **SECTION 1. ACKNOWLEDGEMENT.**

3   That the House of Representatives regrets the pas-
4   sage of legislation that adversely affected people of Chi-
5   nese origin in the United States because of their ethnicity.

•HRES 683 IH

151

5

SEC. 2. DISCLAIMER.

Nothing in this resolution may be construed or relied on to authorize or support any claim, including but not limited to constitutionally based claims, claims for monetary compensation or claims for equitable relief against the United States or any other party, or serve as a settlement of any claim against the United States.

○

v . Chinese Population in the United States (1840-2010)

Year	US Total Population	Chinese	Percentage of Chinese%
1840	17,069,453	not available	n/a
1850	23,191,876	4,018	0.02%
1860	31,443,321	34,933	0.11%
1870	38,558,371	64,199	0.17%
1880	50,189,209	105,465	0.21%
1890	62,979,766	107,488	0.17%
1900	76,212,168	118,746	0.16%
1910	92,228,496	94,414	0.10%
1920	106,021,537	85,202	0.08%
1930	123,202,624	102,159	0.08%
1940	132,164,569	106,334	0.08%
1950	151,325,798	150,005	0.10%
1960	179,323,175	237,292	0.13%
1970	203,302,031	436,062	0.21%
1980	226,542,199	812,178	0.36%
1990	248,709,873	1,645,472	0.66%
2000	281,421,906	2,432,585	0.86%
2010	308,745,538	3,794,673	1.23%

(Source: U.S. Immigration Bureau)

Bibliography

1. Manuscript and Government Document

Committee on Immigration and Naturalization, House of Representatives, 78th Congress, *Samples of Japanese-Controlled Radio Comments on America's Exclusion Act* (confidential print), 1943, National Archives, Washington D.C.

U.S. Congress, House of Representative, Papers of Minutes Committee on Immigration and Naturalization, 1943, National Archives, Washington D.C.

U.S. Congress, House of Representatives, *A Bill to Provide for the Admission to the United States of Alien Chinese Wives of American Citizens*. H.R. 1607, 78th Congress, 1st Session, 1943, Washington D.C.

Confidential U.S. State Department Central Files, United States –China Relations, 1940-1949, Vol. 1, National Archives, Washington D.C.

Daitoa senso kankei ikken: Kakkoku no taido - Chuka minkoku (kokuminseifu) [Files Relating to the Greater East Asia War: The Attitudes of the Governments - The Chinese National Government], Foreign Ministry of Japan, Tokyo.

Franklin D. Roosevelt Papers, Franklin D. Roosevelt Library, Hyde Park, New York.

Papers of Walter H. Judd, Hoover Institution, Stanford University.

Papers of Minutes Committee on Immigration and Naturalization, House of Representatives, U.S. Congress. National Archives, Washington, D.C.

Records of the Citizens Committee to Repeal Chinese Exclusion and Place Immigration on a Quota Basis, New York Public Library, New York.

Records of American Labor Conference on International Affairs: Files of Citizens Committee to Repeal Chinese Exclusion and Place Immigration on a Quota Basis, Tamiment Institute Library, New York University, New York.

Roger S. Greene Papers, Houghton Library, Harvard University.

Senator Hiram Fong Papers, University of Hawaii at Manoa Library, Hawaii.

U.S. Congress, *Congressional Record,* 77th Congress, 2nd Session.

U.S. House of Representatives, *Hearings before the Committee on Immigration and Naturalization, Repeal of the Chinese Exclusion Acts*, 78th Congress, 1st Session, May and June 1943, Washington. D.C.

U.S. Department of State, *Papers Relating to the Foreign Relations of the United States*, 1942 - 1943, Washington D.C.

U.S. Department of State, *Bulletin*, 1942-1943.

Foreign Ministry of Japan, Daitoa senso kankei yikken: Senden no ken, January 1943, Foreign Ministry of Japan, Tokyo.

Foreign Ministry of Japan, ed., *Nippon gaiko bunsho narabini shuyo*

unso [Important Documents on the Foreign Relations of
Japan]. Tokyo, 1969.

Zhongguo Guomingdang Zhongyang Weiyuanhui Dangshi Weiyuanhui
ed., *Zhonghuamingguo Zhongyao Shiliao Chubian: Duiri Kanzhan
Shiqi* [Important Historical Documents of the Republic of
China: During the Period of the Anti-Japanese War]. Taiwan:
Central Book Publishing Co., 1981.

2. Newspapers

Asahi Shimbun

Asia Magazine

Asia and the Americas

Christian Century

The Christian Science Monitor

Chinese Mind

Common Ground

Contemporary China

FRONT

Los Angle Times

The New York Times

San Francisco Chronicle

Toa Kaihou

Washington Post

Zhonghua Ribao

3. Articles and Books

Archdeacon, Thomas J. *Becoming American: An Ethnic History*. New York and London: The Free Press, 1983.

Arnold, Kathleen R. *Anti-Immigration in the United States.* West Port, Connecticut: Greenwood Press, 2011.

Bagby, Wesley Marvin. *The Eagle-Dragon Alliance: America's Relations with China in World War II*. Newark: University of Delaware Press, 1992.

Barde. Robert, and Gustavo J. Bobonis. "Detention at Angel Island: First Empirical Evidence," *Social Science History*, Vol.30, 2006.

Barth, Gunther. *Bitter Strength: A History of the Chinese in the United States.* Cambridge: Harvard University Press, 1964.

Buck, Pearl S. *What America Means to Me*. New York: John Day Co., 1942.

Buck, Pearl S. *American Unity and Asia*. New York: John Day Co, 1942

Chan, Sucheng, ed. *Entry Denied: Exclusion and the Chinese Community in America, 1882-1943*. Philadelphia: Temple University Press, 1991.

Chen, Shehon. *Being Chinese, Becoming Chinese American.* Champaign, Illinois: University of Illinois Press, 2006.

Chen, Yong. *Chinese San Francisco, 1850-1943.* Stanford: Stanford

University Press, 2002.

Chiang, Kai-shek. *China's Destiny*. New York: Macmillan, 1947.

Chin, Gabriel and Hrishi Karthikeyan. "Preserving Racial Identity: Population Patterns and Application or Anti-Miscegenation Statutes to Asian Americans, 1910-1950." *Asian Law Journal*, Vol.19, 2002.

Chung, Sue Fawn. *In Pursuit of Gold: Chinese American Miners and Merchants in the American West*. Champaign, Illinois: University of Illinois Press, 2014.

Cohen, Warren I. *The Chinese Connection: Roger S. Greene, Thomas W. Lamont, George E. Sokolsky and American-East Asian Relations*. New York: Columbia University Press, 1978.

Conn, Peter. *Pearl Buck: A Cultural Biography*. Cambridge: Cambridge University Press, 1996.

Coolidge, Mary R. *Chinese Immigration*. New York, 1909.

Cross, Ira B. *A History of the Labor Movement in California*. Berkeley: California University Press, 1935.

Dallek, Robert. *Franklin D. Roosevelt and American Foreign Policy, 1932-1945*. New York, 1979.

Daniels, Roger. *Asian Americans: Chinese and Japanese in the United States since 1850*. Seattle: University of Washington Press, 1988.

Daniels, Roger, and Otis L. Graham. *Debating American Immigration, 1882-Present*. Lanham, Maryland: Rowan & Littlefield Publishers, 2001.

Daniels, Roger. "No Lamps Were Lit for Them: Angel Island and the Historiography of Asian American Immigration," *Journal of American Ethnic History*, Vol.17, 1991.

Dinnerstein, Leonard, David M. Reimers. *Ethnic Americans: A History of Immigration and Assimilation.* New York: Harper & Row, 1982.

Dower, John. *War without Mercy: Race and Power in the Pacific War.* New York: Pantheon Books, 1986.

Elmer, Sandmeyer. *The Anti-Chinese Movement in California.* Urbana: University of Illinois Press, 1973.

Feingold, Henry L. *The Jewish People in America: A Time for Searching - Entering the Mainstream, 1920-1945.* Baltimore, Maryland: John Hopkins University Press, 1992.

Feis, Herbert. *The China Tangle: The American Effort from Pearl Harbor to the Marshall Mission.* Princeton, NJ: Princeton University Press, 1953.

Finney, Charles G. *The Old China Hands.* Westport, Connecticut: Greenwood Press, 1973.

Freedman, Russell. *Angel Island, Gateway to Gold Mountain.* London: Clarion Books, 2014.

Gao, Yanli. "Judd's China: A Missionary Congressman and US-China Policy," *Journal of Modern Chinese History*, December 2008.

Garson, Robert A. and Stuart S. Kidd eds. *The Roosevelt Years: New Perspectives on American History, 1933-1945.* Edinburgh:

Edinburgh University Press, 1999.

Garzer, Nathan. *Ethnic Dilemmas 1964-1982*. Cambridge: Harvard University Press, 1983.

Gilmore, Allison B. *You Can't Fight Tanks with Bayonets: Psychological Warfare against the Japanese Army in the Southwest Pacific*. Lincoln: University of Nebraska Press, 1998.

Glick, Clarence Elmer. *Sojourners and Settlers, Chinese Migrants in Hawaii*. Honolulu: University of Hawaii Press, 1980.

Gold, Martin B. *Forbidden Citizens: Chinese Exclusion and the U.S. Congress: A Legislative History*. Washington D.C.: TheCapitol.Net, 2012.

Gyory, Andrew. *Closing the Gate: Race, Politics and the Chinese Exclusion Act*. Chapel Hill, NC: University of North Carolina Press, 1998.

Heinrichs, Waldo. *Threshold War: Franklin D. Roosevelt and American Entry into World War II*. Oxford and New York: Oxford University Press, 1988.

Higham, John. *Stranger in the Land: Patterns of American Nativism since 1860-1925*. New Brunswick, NJ: Rutgers University Press, 1994.

Hing, Bill Ong. *Making and Remaking Asian America through Immigration Policy, 1850-1990*. Stanford: Stanford University Press, 1993.

Hsu, Madeline. *Dreaming of Gold, Dreaming of Home:*

Trans-nationalism and Migration between the United States and South China, 1882-1943. Stanford: Stanford University Press, 2000.

Hsu, Madeline. *The Good Immigrants: How the Yellow Peril Became the Model Minority*. Princeton: Princeton University Press, 2015.

Hutchinson, Edward P. *Legislative History of American Immigration Policy, 1798-1965.* Philadelphia: University of Pennsylvania Press, 1981.

Iriye, Akira. *American, Chinese, and the Japanese Perspective on Wartime Asia, 1931-1949*. Wilmington, Delaware: A Scholarly Resources Imprint, 1990.

Iriye, Akira. *The Origins of the Second World War in Asia and the Pacific.* London and New York: Longman, 1987.

Iriye, Akira. *Power and Culture: The Japanese-American War, 1941-1945*. Cambridge: Harvard University Press, 1981.

Izumi, Hirobe. *Japanese Pride, American Prejudice: Modifying the Exclusion Clause of the 1924 Immigration Act*. Stanford: Stanford University Press, 2002.

Lee, Edwards. *Missionary for Freedom: The Life and Times of Walter Judd.* New York: Paragon, 1990.

Lee, Erika. *At America's Gates: Chinese Immigration during the Exclusion Era, 1882-1943*. Chapel Hill: University of North Carolina Press, 2003.

Lee, Marjorie. *Duty & Honor a Tribute to Chinese American World War*

II Veterans of Southern. San Francisco: Chinese Historical Society,
1998.

Lepore, Herbert P. *Anti-Asian Exclusion in the United States during the
Nineteenth Century and the Twentieth Centuries: The History
Leading to the Immigration Act of 1924.* Lewiston, New York:
Edwin Mellen Press, 2013.

Li, Tien-lu. *Congressional Policy on Chinese Immigration.* New York:
Arno Press, 1978.

Lipscomb J. Elizabeth J. ed. *The Several World of Pearl S. Buck.*
Westport, Conn: Westwood Press, 1994.

Lum, Arlene. *Sailing for the Sun: The Chinese in Hawaii 1789-1989.*
The Three Heroes, 1990.

Ma, Xiaohua. "The Invisible War between the United States and Japan: A
Study of the Abolition of Extraterritoriality in 1943," *The Journal
of American and Canadian Studies*, Vol. 15, 1997.

Ma, Xiaohua. "A Democracy at War: The American Campaign to Repeal
Chinese Exclusion in 1943," *Journal of American Studies* Vol.8,
1998.

Ma, Xiaohua. *Maboroshi no shinchitsujo to ajia taiheiyo: Dainiji seikai
taisenki no beichu domei no atsureki* [Illusionary Orders in the
Asia-Pacific: The Chinese American Alliance in the War against
Japan. Tokyo: Sairyuusha, 2000.

Mackerras, Colin. *Western Images of China.* Oxford: Oxford University
Press, 1989.

May, Ernest R. *American-East Asian Relations: A Survey.* Cambridge: Harvard University Press, 1972.

McClain, Charles J. *In Search of Equality: The Chinese Struggle against Discrimination in Nineteenth-Century America.* Berkeley: University of California Press, 1994.

Mckee, Delber L. *Chinese Exclusion versus the Open Door Policy.* Cambridge: Harvard University Press, 1963.

Moy, Victoria. *Fighting for the Dream: Voices of Chinese American Veterans from World War II to Afghanistan.* Los Angles: Chinese Historical Society of Southern California, 2014.

Najia, Aarim-Heriot. *Chinese Immigrants, African Americans, and Racial Anxiety in the United States, 1848-82.* Champaign, Illinois: University of Illinois Press, 2006.

Niiya, Bria. ed. *Japanese American History.* Los Angeles: The Japanese American National Museum, Facts on File, Inc., 1996.

Railton, Benjamin. *The Chinese Exclusion Act: What It Can Teach Us about America.* New York: Palgrave Pivot, 2013.

Reeves, Richard. Infamy: *The Shocking Story of the Japanese American Internment in World War II.* New York: Henry Hold and Co., 2015.

Riggs, Fred W. *Pressures on Congress: A Study of the Repeal of Chinese Exclusion.* New York: King's Crown Press, 1950.

Robert, McClellan. *The Heathen Chinese: A Study of American Attitudes toward China, 1890-1905.* Columbus, Ohio: Ohio State University Press, 1971.

Sandmeyer, Elmer. *The Anti-Chinese Movement in California.* Champaign: University of Illinois Press, 1991.

Saxton, Alexander. *The Indispensable Enemy: Labor and the Anti-Chinese Movement in California.* Berkeley: University of California Press, 1975.

Seagrave, Sterling. *The Soong Dynasty.* New York: Harper & Row, Publishers, 1986.

Schaller, Michael. *The U.S. Crusade in China, 1938-1945.* New York: Columbia University Press, 1979.

Sherwood, Robert E. *Roosevelt and Hopkins: An Intimate History.* New York, 1948.

Smith, Stacey L. *Freedom's Frontier: California and the Struggle over Unfree Labor, Emancipation, and Reconstruction.* Chapel Hill: University of North Carolina Press, 2013.

Stuart, Miller. *The Unwelcome Immigrant: The American Image of the Chinese, 1785-1882.* Berkeley: University of California Press, 1969.

Stilwell, Joseph W. *The Stilwell Papers.* New York, 1948.

Sutter, Robert G.. *U.S.-China Relations: Perilous Past, Pragmatic Present.* Lanham, Maryland: Rowman & Littlefield Publishers, 2013.

Takaki, Ronald. *Strangers from a Different Shore: A History of Asian Americans.* Boston: Little Brown & Co., 1989.

Tang, Tsou. *America's Failure in China, 1941-1950.* Chicago:

University of Chicago Press, 1963.

Thorne, Christopher. *Allies of a Kind: The United States, Britain, and the War against Japan, 1941-1945*. London: Hamish Hamilton Ltd, 1982.

Thorne, Christopher. *The Issues of War: States, Society, and the Far Eastern Conflict of 1941-1945*. London, 1989.

Thornton, Jeremy. *The Gold Rush: Chinese Immigrants Come to America 1848-1882*. New York: Rosen Publishing Groups, 2004.

Tsai, Shih-Shan Henry. *The Chinese Experience in America*. Bloomington: Indiana University Press, 1986.

Tsai, Shih-shan Henry. *China and the Overseas Chinese in the United States, 1868-1911*. Fayetteville: University of Arkansas Press, 1983.

Vary, Paul A. *The Closing of the Door: Sino-American Relations, 1936-1946*. East Lansing: Michigan State University Press, 1973.

Williams, T. Harry. ed., *Hayes: The Diary of a President, 1875-1881*. New York, 1964.

Wong, K. Scott. *Americans First: Chinese Americans and the Second World War*. Philadelphia, Pennsylvania: Temple University Press, 2008.

Wu, Ju-lun, ed., *Li weng zhong gon quanji* [Complete Works of Li Hong-zhang] Vol. 8.Taibei, 1962.

Wu, Chen-tsu. *"Chink!": A Documentary History of Anti-Chinese Prejudice in America*. New York: Oceana Publication Inc., 1972.

Yee, Pau. *Tales from Gold Mountain: Stories of the Chinese in the New World.* Toronto: Greenwood Books, 2003.

Yong, Elliott. *Alien Nation: Chinese Migration in the Americas from Coolie Era through World War II.* Chapel Hills: North Carolina University Press, 2014.

Young, Arthur N. *China and the Helping Hand, 1937-1945.* Cambridge: Harvard University Press, 1963.

Yung, Judy, and Gordon H. Chang, eds. *Chinese American Voices: From the Gold Rush to the Present.* Berkeley: University of California Press, 2006.

Zhang Yu-fa, ed., *Zhongguo Xiandaishi Lunji* [Selected Works on Modern Chinese History] Vol.9. Taibei, 1982.

Zo, Kil Young. *Chinese Emigration into the United States, 1850-1880.* New York: Arno Press, 1978.

Chinese American Memory of World War II

2015年8月30日　発行

著　者　馬暁華
発行所　学術研究出版／ブックウェイ
　　　　〒670-0933　姫路市平野町62
　　　　TEL.079 (222) 5372　FAX.079 (223) 3523
　　　　http://bookway.jp
印刷所　小野高速印刷株式会社
©Xiaohua Ma 2015, Printed in Japan
ISBN978-4-86584-053-7

乱丁本・落丁本は送料小社負担でお取り換えいたします。

本書のコピー、スキャン、デジタル化等の無断複製は著作権法上での例外を除き
禁じられています。本書を代行業者等の第三者に依頼してスキャンやデジタル化
することは、たとえ個人や家庭内の利用でも一切認められておりません。